Christopher Columbus
and the European Discovery of America

Christopher Columbus and the European Discovery of America.

Robert Hume

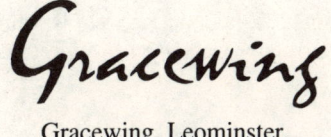

Gracewing, Leominster.

First Published in 1992

Gracewing
Fowler Wright Books
Southern Ave, Leominster
Herefordshire HR6 0QF

Gracewing Books are distributed

In New Zealand by
Catholic Supplies Ltd
80 Adelaide Rd
Wellington
New Zealand

In Australia by
Charles Paine Pty
8 Ferris Street
North Parramatta
NSW 2151 Auatralia

In Canada by
Novalis
P. O. Box 990
Outremont H2V 457
Canada

In USA by
Morehouse Publishing
P.O. Box 1321
Harrisburg
PA 17105
U. S. A.

© *Text* Dr. Robert Hume.

© *Illustrations* Various, see acknowledgements.

Typesetting by   Orphans Printing Press
                   Hereford Road
                   Leominster
                   Herefordshire

Printed and bound in Great Britain by
Billings and Son Ltd., Worcester

ISBN 0 85244 2114

iv

CONTENTS

LIST OF ILLUSTRATIONS

1. Imaginary sea monsters
2. The Viking route from Greenland to North America
3. The Altissimo Portrait of Columbus
4. Columbus in middle age
5. The Paulus Jovius Portrait of Columbus
6. The Thevet Portrait
7. Genoa, from the *Nuremberg Chronicle (1493)*
8. Public monument to Columbus in Piazza Ovetto, Genoa
9. Columbus's house in Piazza Dante, Genoa
10. Columbus's strange signature
11. Queen Isabella by an unknown artist
12. The Grand Khan
13. Columbus leaving the King and Queen on the shore of Spain
14. The *Landing of Columbus,* 12 October, 1492
15. Building a fort at La Navidad, Española
16. The route of Columbus's first voyage, 1492-3
17. Cannibals
18. The route of Columbus's second voyage, 1493-6
19. Christopher and Bartholomew Columbus are arrested and enchained
20. The route of Columbus's third voyage, 1498-1500
21. The route of Columbus's fourth voyage, 1502-4
22. Columbus's men plant a cross on Española
23. Indians sowing maize
24. Columbus's men discover the Indians smoking tobacco
25. The origins of Columbus's legacy
26. The 'triangular trade'
27. The first bronze statue of Columbus in the U.S.A.

ACKNOWLEDGEMENTS

The author and publisher would like to thank the following for permission to reproduce illustrations:

The *Galleria degli Uffizi, Firenze* and George Weidenfeld & Nicolson Limited (Plate 3); the 'Architect of the Capitol' (Front cover and Plate 14); the Rare Books and Manuscripts Division, The New York Public Library, Astor, Lenox and Tilden Foundations (Plate 13); the Royal Collection, St. James's Palace (Plate 11); The Mansell Collection (Plate 15); and the *Civico Museo Archeologico "Giovio", Como* (Plate 4). Plates 1, 5, 6, 7, 12, 17, 19, 22, 23 and 24 all appear 'By Permission of the British Library'; and Plate 27 courtesy of John Karel, Director of Tower Grove Park Archives, St Louis, Missouri, U.S.A.

The author and publisher would also like to thank Random House Inc., (publishers) New York, for permission to quote from Jack Weatherford's *Indian Givers* (1988).

Chapter I

The World Before Columbus

The exotic taste for mystery and legend, shared by the rich in medieval times, was fed by the many beautifully illustrated maps, engraved by hand on vellum. It is tempting to think that because some six hundred of these large and intriguingly illuminated manuscripts were produced between the eighth and fifteenth centuries, steady progress was being made throughout these years in our knowledge of the world. But this was not in fact the case, for medieval maps were more likely to be items of admiration, wonder and curiosity, than of accuracy. Although the demand for maps sometimes came from those interested in commerce and conquest, most were acquired for show rather than for use, just as today someone might buy a reproduction of an old master.

Hundreds of fabulous names such as the Hesperides and Elysian Fields loom up out of Seas of Darkness, into which gush mythical rivers delicately coloured in gold. To utilise the space and give good value for money, they were crammed with purely fanciful islands, fanned by the breath of the gods. These islands were shown well away from land, thereby further reducing the apparent size of the ocean. One of the best known of these, usually shown surrounded by mist just west of the Canaries, was the island of Saint Brandan. Exhaustive attempts to locate it failed so that it eventually became known as the Lost Isle; but it was still being shown on maps as late as the nineteenth century.

These so-called 'cloister maps' were never intended to be used by travellers or traders, for they were produced by monks, acting as cartographers, whose concerns were philosophical rather than scientific. Their main concern was to place Jerusalem at the centre of the picture, thereby drawing attention to its importance. Naturally, travellers and traders had their own more practical nautical guides and charts, called Portolans; but even these were likely to contain imaginary islands, legendary sea-monsters and biblical stories such as that of Gog and Magog.

The disc-shaped world map (1275-1317) in Hereford Cathedral is now perhaps the most famous of all medieval maps. Here fact and fiction are closely connected: Julius Caesar co-exists with mermaids, unicorns, dragons and four-eyed Ethiopians. In trying to bring the map into harmony with the Bible it depicts Paradise, the Garden of Eden, the Last Judgment, and even Satan taking the condemned away to punishment.

Very few people, even as late as the end of the fourteenth century, were willing to accept that the earth was round; and Columbus himself believed - uniquely, it seems - that it was pear-shaped. Even some of those who *were* convinced argued that vessels returning from voyages round the world would have to sail up slopes as steep as the Swiss Alps.

It was not until the fifteenth century - Columbus's own time - that map-making really began to improve, fuelled by the feverish spirit of enquiry associated with the Renaissance, and stimulated by the invention of printing in Germany. Centuries before, in Egypt, Ptolemy had produced maps which now underwent something of a revival and provided the basis for exciting new ideas.

Medieval man knew little about his world, for people were unlikely to travel outside their own parish in an age when journeys were difficult and dangerous. Indeed we probably know more about the moon today than people living at that time knew about the earth. The handful of people who travelled outside Europe usually made their way eastwards to India or China where they hoped to find, not merely immense riches, such as gold, precious stones and spices, but also adventure and excitement in uncharted lands. In this way they were inspired by Marco Polo, who travelled overland from Italy to China during the thirteenth century and on his return told amazing stories about the wealth of distant rulers. One of Marco Polo's claims was that 'All the world's monarchs put together have not such riches as the Great Khan'. His was one of the most popular books of the time, and we know that Columbus had his own copy.

Travellers fabricated tales about giants, dwarfs, dragons and monsters, knowing that few would be able to disprove what they said. The fantastic tales which appeared under the name of Sir John de Mandeville were especially widely read. Here we meet animals - such as giraffes, elephants and crocodiles - which were unknown to Europeans. It was also believed that there existed a rare species of man-eating ants, each the size of a hound, which lived in huge hills where they spent their time refining gold. Horrific human deformities were everywhere to be found. In the desert, for instance, lived wild men with horns, hideous to look at and unable to make more than a grunting noise. Elsewhere were people whose ears hung down to their knees, or whose lips were so big that they could be curled up and used as sun shades.

Remote islands provided an especially rich seam of stories. On one, close to India, could be found terrifying giants with one eye in the middle of their forehead who lived off a diet of raw flesh and fish.

The natives of another had no heads, eyes in their shoulders, and a crooked mouth in the shape of a horseshoe in their chest. On yet another island could be found people with completely flat faces, with just two holes for eyes and no nose or mouth.

Travellers believed that the Northern Ocean was clogged with salt and covered with ice. It was infamous for its terrible whirlpools, like the Maelstrom, which could suck in ships and disgorge them again like a gigantic sea monster. One English friar, writing in 1364, claimed that the four seas met at the North Pole, which explained why the currents were so strong there. Once a ship reached this point it was doomed, for it would now be drawn towards the Pole itself - a huge, black, magnetic rock - where it would be smashed to pieces.

If you dared travel south, and were lucky enough to get past the ferocious Muslim pirates of North Africa, you might well encounter the man-eating sea monster called the Kraken, or the griffin (half-eagle, half-lion), whose claws were big enough to carry a man and a horse away and crush his very bones. Beyond this lay an area called the Torrid Zone, where the sea was so hot that it boiled. Here the ship's tar would melt and the ship would be burnt to cinders. The sailors would be sucked beneath the bubbling sea where, screaming with agony, they would suffer a terrible death.

1. Imaginary sea monster
[woodcut from Sebastian Munster's *Cosmographia* (1550)]

If you sailed too far west on the perilous Great Sea of Perpetual Darkness you would eventually fall off the edge of the world at the point where the ocean flowed over it in an endless waterfall; that is, of course, if you had not already been swallowed up by another gigantic monster, called 'The Bishop of the Sea' to signify its total authority.

In the extreme east a 'Terrestrial Paradise' was believed to exist, or so Sir John de Mandeville claimed. Here travellers could drink from the

Fountain of Eternal Youth and stay fit and young for evermore. This was in direct contrast to the water in the wells of Africa, which was so cold during the day that it was impossible to drink and so hot at night that it scalded your throat. Little wonder, perhaps, that the inhabitants sometimes turned blue; but it is difficult to reconcile this with the other belief, that they had one enormous foot.

These horrific tales must inevitably have influenced the attitudes of seamen; and as if these fears were not enough to contend with, the ships themselves presented practical difficulties. Short and broad (no more than 80 foot by 28 foot), they provided little room for the crew, supplies and equipment. At best they were suitable for sailing in the Mediterranean and the coastal waters of the Atlantic from Iceland to West Africa.

Sailors were simply not used to sailing out of the sight of land for more than a few days at a time. With only a single large mainsail, they needed a safe harbour or anchorage if they were not to be dashed to pieces. Leaks were virtually an everyday event, so that the crew spent much of their time manning the pumps. The ships' timber offered a great home for sea-worms since it was prone to rot. The decks had to be kept damp, for if they dried out in the extreme heat of the tropics they would crack. Sails and ropes had to be repaired frequently, and there were many fatal accidents. Another dangerous job for the unwary seaman was attending to the rudder which took a continual beating from the waves.

Sailors found their way by following the coastline and keeping watch for well-known landmarks. They were desperately afraid of the unknown. On entering the harbour at Pisa, a medieval pilot-book advised: 'when the end of the harbour appears between two towers, follow that way and you will go clear of all the rocks'. But in the oceans at large known landfalls were pitifully few.

Navigational 'technology', as such, was extremely primitive. When it came down to it, sailing was a matter of calculated guesswork. There were no chronometers and though an astrolabe could be used to work out latitude it was really a land instrument and ships were rarely still enough for an accurate reading. As for reckoning the passage of time, it depended on one of the ship's boys remembering to turn the sand-glass every hour or half-hour. For working out speed and distance it was helpful to know the number of leagues normally sailed in one turn of the sand glass, but sailors were ultimately forced to rely on observation and experience. Usually this was done by throwing a piece of driftwood overboard, or by watching pieces of seaweed float by; but this was a rough and ready guide in view of all the currents, and seamen were recommended to make two estimates of speed if they were to avoid being shipwrecked. Though there were compasses to tell direction, nothing was really understood about magnetic variation. Sailors would simply say that the needle 'north-easted' or 'north-wested' and leave it at that. Some might think it was due to a poor lodestone (magnet), or a badly hung needle; others that the ship was drifting off course without their realising it.

Powerful currents and the weather were forever taking the sailors by surprise. Few ships could sail in a direction other than the one the wind took them. One of the greatest worries was that the wind might blow the ship directly towards a nearby coast. Far safer, when approaching an unknown shore in the late afternoon, was to drop anchor for the night. If you wished to sail due west, for most of the year you were prevented from doing so by the strength of the Westerlies. Coping with intimidating gale-force winds like the Roaring Forties, which would tear at the mast, and finding oneself becalmed in tranquil seas were totally new experiences.

Finally, lack of supplies were a perpetual problem. Fresh water soon turned slimy and foul, and ran out quickly. Other provisions had to be preserved in salt. Heavily salted food was unpalatable; so were biscuits ridden with maggots. Shortage of fresh fruit and vegetables led to scurvy, and poor sanitation brought pneumonia, dysentery and T.B., usually fatal in those days.

It is little wonder therefore that crews spent a great deal of time anxiously looking for signs of land - a floating branch, certain birds, low-lying cloud and changes in the colour of the sea. Though sightings often turned out to be false alarms, any of these would help to raise the men's flagging spirits; but when they saw nothing for days on end it was natural enough for them to lose confidence and be tempted to doubt their captain, even to the point of mutiny.

1492 is usually considered a watershed in history. Before this time, it is claimed, there were two worlds, totally unaware of each other. Suddenly this parallel existence came to an end, the dividing line was crossed and contacts were made.

Twenty-five thousand years before America's original settlers had arrived. They had begun their journey in Asia and had crossed Siberia and Alaska. These native American Indians, who numbered between eight and ten million by Columbus's time, were the *real* discoverers of America.

There had also been a number of intermittent visits to the New World before Columbus. The problem is that some of these visits are conjectural and the facts are contained within heavily-embroidered tales involving abnormal phenomena, such as one-legged people and sea monsters.

Some of these tales can be dismissed out of hand. For example, the Chinese must surely have reached Japan rather than Mexico in the fifth century, and though the Irish certainly reached Iceland there is no archaeological proof whatever of an Irish colony in America in the seventh century.

Three hundred years before Columbus a Welsh Prince called Madoc visited America, or so it was claimed in one tale, and founded colonies somewhere between Newfoundland and Mexico. Finding the land so attractive, it is said he took out a large band of men who taught the Indians to speak Welsh. This kind of wishful-thinking, for which there is not a shred of evidence, may well have been invented to make British claims to possession more legitimate.

The voyages of the Northmen, on the other hand, in the first two decades of the eleventh century are more believable. Though they disagree on detail, they are certainly supported in essence by narrative evidence both from *The Greenlanders' Saga* (c.1200) and from *Erik the Red's Saga* (c.1270). Some writers have dismissed the sagas as no more than fairy tales based on oral tradition, but archaeological finds in Greenland certainly fit in well, and many of the details in the sagas about vegetation and animal life can be corroborated.

In all probability America was indeed first rediscovered by the Vikings. In the mid-eighth century they were already sailing to England, Scotland and Ireland. By the middle of the next century they had reached Iceland, and shortly after they arrived at the (to them) aptly named Greenland. The first sighting of America is attributed to Bjarni Herjolfsson, whose ship was blown off course on his journey from Iceland to Greenland and, some three days later, was driven south into an unknown foggy area of ocean. After the fog had cleared up, he saw the shores, low hills and forests of a strange land. This was not Greenland, as he at first supposed, but the New World. Missing two opportunities of going ashore, no doubt through fear, he returned home, leaving it to another to claim the land.

It was one of the sons of Eric the Red, Leif Ericsson, in the eleventh century, who was determined to take Bjarni's initiative further. *The Greenlanders' Saga* tells us:

> About this time, there began to be much talk... that Wineland the Good should be explored, for, it was said, that country must be possessed of many goodly qualities. And so it came to pass, that Karlsefni and Snorri fitted out their ship, for the purpose of going in search of that country in the spring. Bjarni and Thorhall joined the expedition with their ship...They had in all one hundred and sixty men... Then they saw land, and launched a boat, and explored the land, and found there large flat stones... there were many Arctic foxes there. They gave a name to the country, and called it Helluland [Labrador]. Then they sailed with northerly winds... and land then lay before them, and upon it was a great wood and many wild beasts... the land where the wood was they called Markland or Forest-land [Newfoundland].

A colony was founded and duly given the name Vinland [Nova Scotia] because of the grapes (or perhaps berries) to be found there. In 1001 he returned to Greenland with a cargo of timber, and his experiences kindled the imagination of others. Next year his brother, Thorvald,

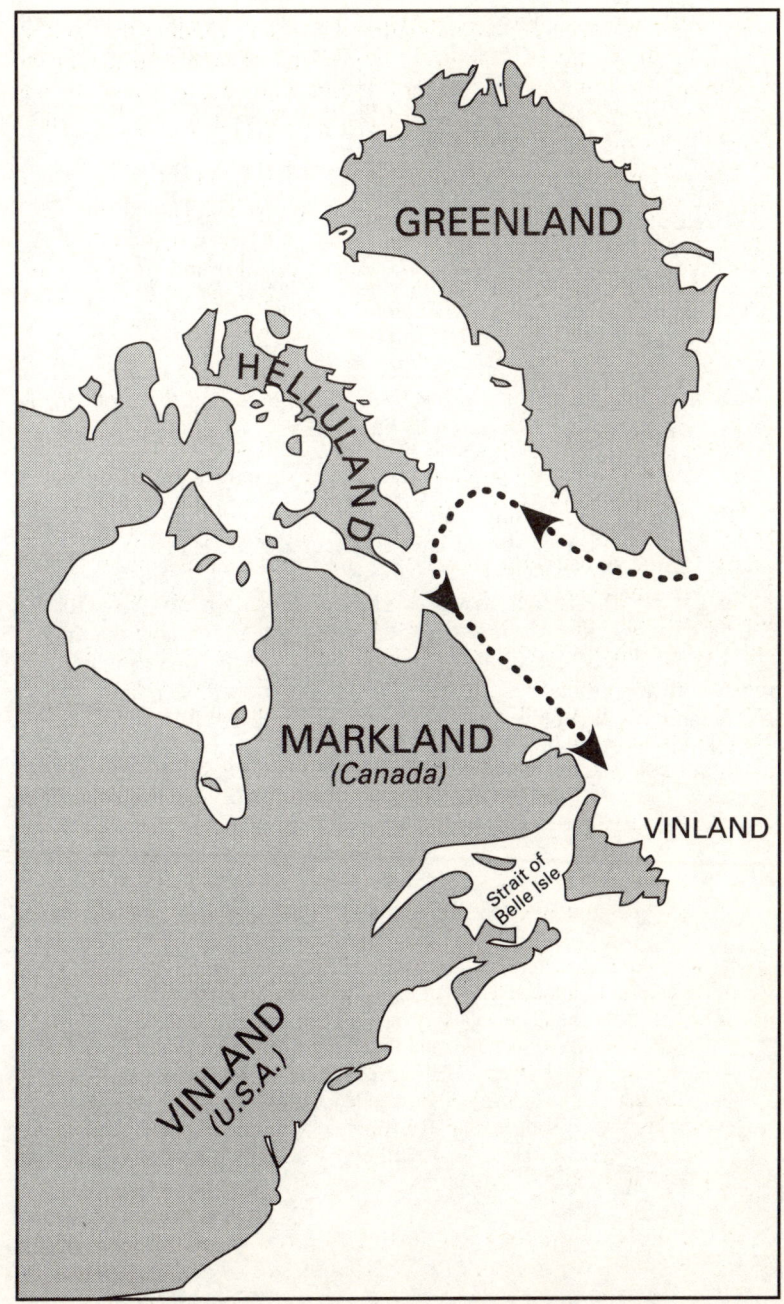

2. The route taken by the Vikings from Greenland to North America

sailed to Vinland, explored its western coastline and then travelled north in the direction of Markland, but he was killed either by American Indians, or perhaps by Skraelings (Eskimos).

In a particularly gruesome voyage in 1011 some sixty-five men sailed for Vinland under the leadership of two brothers, Helgi and Finnbogi, and Leif's sister Freydis, with her husband Thorvard. Their aim was not to found a colony but to cut down timber, but very soon the leaders began to quarrel and Thorvard, on the orders of Freydis, struck the brothers down in cold blood outside their own huts. After this, probably because of the hostility of the natives, the Vikings abandoned their settlements and made no further attempts to explore or colonise Vinland.

An Icelandic geography (c.1160) gives us exciting details of these new American lands and supports the idea that Helluland lay to the south of Greenland, that next to it can be found Markland and that not too far away is Vinland the Good. Eight hundred years later the Norwegian archaeologist Helge Ingstad excavated fifteen occupation sites near the entrance to the Strait of Belle Isle (see map) and found large buildings with many rooms, including halls and boat sheds, constructed in a Viking style. That the Vikings should have discovered America is scarcely surprising. Their experiences on the stormy waters west of Norway would have forced them to learn navigation. Here, in contrast to the Mediterranean, sailors were often out of sight of land for days at a time.

Thus we can be certain that Columbus was not the first to rediscover the American continent : Leif Ericsson and others had been there almost five hundred years before him. But the Viking voyages did not lead to the opening up of the Americas. It was left to Christopher Columbus to leave his mark on history by paving the way for the first European settlement.

Chapter II

The Unknown Columbus

Much about Columbus is shrouded in mystery. Not least there is the problem of his physical appearance. Though there are more than eighty portraits of the man, none of them was painted during his lifetime. Apart from the aquiline nose, each portrait is different. Some show a long face, others an oval face, still others a beard.

Altissimo's portrait in the Uffizi, Florence, shows a sombre, ghostly, figure with a pallid complexion, sunken eyes and straggly hair [Plate 3]. Closest to it is the fuller-faced, middle-aged, figure preserved today at Como [Plate 4]. Quite different is De Bry's engraving (1595) depicting a man with a round face, large eyes and thick black curly hair. It bears no similarity at all to the friendlier Jovius [Plate 5] and Villa Doria portraits, showing a man with a prominent dimple on his chin. Though most of the figures are clean-shaven, there are about half a dozen bearded examples, the most famous of which is the Thevet portrait [Plate 6]. In contrast is the effeminate Lombard work at Naples which depicts a rather delicate and reserved courtier. Many of these portraits, however, are not simply imaginative; they are quite impossible. The fanciful Rinck portrait, for

3. The Altissimo Portrait of Columbus (16th century)

4. Columbus in middle age

5. The Paulus Jovius Portrait of Columbus, the oldest known portrait [reported in J. B. Thacher *Christopher Columbus : His Life, His Works, His Remains* (1903)]

6. The Thevet Portrait [reproduced in Thacher (1903)]

example, shows Columbus in the costume of a nineteenth century Canadian fur-trapper.

When we turn to contemporary written descriptions, there is fortunately far greater agreement. Trivigiano, who knew Columbus personally, described him as 'a man of tall and lofty stature, of ruddy complexion... and with a long face' [*Libretto*]. Oviedo, the historian of the Indies, remarks that Columbus

> was of good stature and appearance, of more than medium height and with strong limbs, his eyes bright [a great contrast to the Uffizi portrait] and his other features of good proportion: his hair very red and his face somewhat burned and freckled.

[*Historia General y Natural de Las Indias* (1535) II Ch.2]

The sixteenth century priest Bartolomé de Las Casas was a youth when Columbus returned from the New World. He knew him well, even though he wrote down his observations much later in life:

> His form was tall, above the medium: his face long and his countenance imposing: his nose was aquiline: his eyes clear blue: his complexion light, tending toward a decided red: his beard and hair were red when he was young, but which cares then had early turned white.

[*Historia*, I Ch.2]

Columbus's son, Ferdinand, bears out this description almost exactly:

> The Admiral was a man of good form, of more than medium stature: with a long visage, the cheek-bones a little high: inclining neither to stoutness nor thinness: his nose was aquiline and his eyes light: he was a blond inclining to high colouring: in his youth his hair was fair, but when he was thirty, it had all turned white.
>
> [*Historie* (1571) fol. recto 7]

In addition to discrepancies over his physical appearance there is immense controversy surrounding his birth and early years.

The Italian seaport of Genoa exudes Columbus's presence. The visitor is barely outside the main railway station when he introduces himself, towering over scenes from the voyages from his pedestal in the Piazza Ovetto. The monument's bold dedication confirms his Italian origins: 'To Christopher Columbus from the home country'.

Passing through Via Balbi you reach Via Garibaldi. Here, in the Palazzo del Commune, the Admiral of the Ocean Sea peers down once again, map in hand, this time from a splendid portrait in the Reunion

7, Genoa, from the *Nuremberg Chronicle* (1493)

8. Public monument to Columbus in Piazza Ovetto, Genoa (1862)

Room. Nearby, in the Piazza de Ferrari, is the remarkable but rather garish 'Countdown 92' timepiece outside the Banco di Roma. It bleeps away the seconds while its large red fluorescent numerals count down to 12 October 1992, the 500th anniversary of the landing of Genoa's famous son at San Salvador and the stimulus for the whole Columbus Expo '92.

In the Via Dante Columbus remains ever present. Now he watches you from the corners of commemorative postcards for sale in the pavement kiosks. Each one is proudly captioned 'Genova, città di Colombo'. Soon you emerge into Piazza Dante. In one corner of the busy square, next to the Soprana Gate, you suddenly stumble on Columbus's house. It is difficult not to be taken aback, surrounded as you are by banks, insurance companies and two twenty-five storey skyscrapers. But directly opposite is the 'galleria C.Colombo', the Columbus road tunnel. There is no mistake - you have arrived.

The house, made from stone and bedecked in creeper, is situated on an incline leading up towards the Gate and the Via Ravecca historical centre. It kindles the imagination. This is the very area where Christopher would have played as a child, returning to it at night with tales told him by sailors at the harbour.

The partly obscured tablet seems convincing enough:

NULLA DOMUS TITULO DIGNIOR
HEIC
PATERNIS IN AEDIBUS
CHRISTOPHORUS COLUMBUS
PUERITIAM
PRIMANQUE IUVENTAM TRANSEGIT

['No house better than this one deserves the title of being the paternal home where Christopher Columbus spent his childhood and the first part of his youth']

But in truth, Columbus's origins are obscure. There is no evidence to suggest that this really was Columbus's house. In fact over the years there have been several houses in Genoa, each of which has staked a claim. As the Italian historian Gianni Granzotto (1984) admits, it is just as likely to be 'the product of a patriotic fantasy'.

This uncertainty has opened the way for ten other nations - including France, Spain, Portugal, even Corsica - to claim Columbus's birth rights. Within Italy itself, nineteen different towns have also staked a claim, from Piacenza to Modena.

Though traditionally most biographers have conceded that Columbus was probably born in Genoa, strong counter arguments have been put forward this century that he was Spanish. According to these, the Cristoforo Colombo found in the archives at Genoa is someone quite irrelevant to the study of the New World - 'a downright falsification', as one biogra-

9. Columbus's house in Piazza Dante, Genoa

pher has put it, by over-zealous, patriotic Italian historians. This man Colombo, runs the argument, lived all his life in Genoa and Savona, working as a woolmaker and a bartender. It was quite another man, a Spaniard called Colón, who discovered America. Colón came from a family which owned property around the port of Pontevedra in Galicia, where he was probably born. The name of his mother's family, the Fonterossas, can be found in local records. These Spanish origins would, above all, explain why Colón always wrote in Spanish - to his son and brother, to the ambassador of Genoa and even to an Italian monk.

The Spanish evidence, in my view, is far from convincing, and is riddled with national pride and publicity-seeking. One biographer, Maurice David (1933), subtitled his book *A Sensational Discovery among the Archives of Spain* and aimed to establish definitively 'the true race, real nationality and rightful name of the discoverer of the New World'. Here we encounter the problem of falsification of evidence, for David was relying on the work of the historian García de la Riega who, we now know, forged his Pontevedra documents.

Let us reconsider the idea that Columbus was born in Genoa. Such was certainly the view of most contemporaries. A Spanish court register, pre-dating his first voyage, describes him as 'Cristóbal Colón, genoves'. The Lombard chronicler Martire refers in 1493 to 'a certain Christopher Columbus, Ligurian'. The historians Bernáldez and Las Casas both say he came from Genoa. Oviedo had also been told that he came from the province of Liguria, though possibly from one of the smaller places around Genoa such as Savona or Nevri.

Recently the Italian government and the city of Genoa have taken pains to amass convincing documentary evidence in support of Columbus's Genoese origins. The deeds on display in the 'Sala Colombiana' at the Genoa State Archives confirm not only that there was a Colombo family living in Genoa in the late fifteenth century, but that the father, Domenico, had two sons: first Cristoforo, and later Bartolomeo. In September 1470 we see Domenico and Cristoforo Colombo making an agreement about a debt. Next month a document mentions their receiving a stock of wine, and helps us compute a date for Columbus's birth as some time before 31 October 1451. Two years later, Christopher, now aged twenty-one and described as a wool-draper, is living a few miles away at Savona. Then comes the most exciting document of all, a deed of 25 August 1479, drawn up on the very eve of his departure for Lisbon. Here it specifically says that Columbus was a Genoese citizen with an interest in Madeira sugar, and narrows down his birth to between 26 August and 30 August 1451.

But this may not prove very much. Colombo is a common enough Italian name, and it may have been a coincidence that the names of the brothers were Christopher and Bartholomew. The fact that Columbus is silent about family and friends in Genoa has cast doubt on his Genoese origins. This argument, too, is not conclusive. Columbus may simply have been embarrassed by his humble background.

Salvador de Madariaga (1939) has put forward the theory that the Columbus family only came to settle in Genoa in about 1390, and that they were Catalan Jews. There is no evidence of a Jewish quarter as such in Genoa at this time, but if these were indeed Columbus's origins it would be further reason for him to keep silent about them.

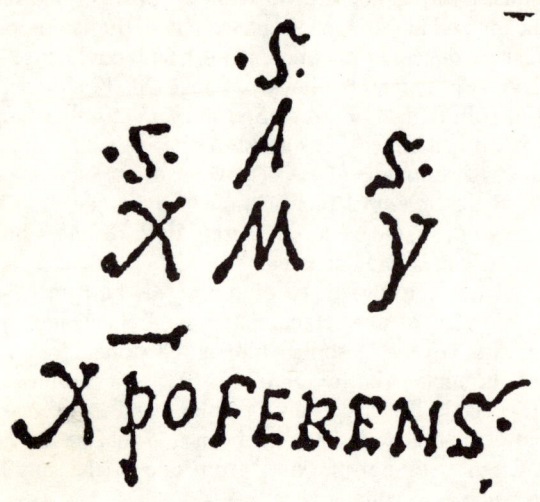

10. Columbus's strange cipher signature

It might also account for the way in which the historian Las Casas talks guardedly of Columbus's Christianity, and help to explain his fascination with the Old Testament in his log and letters. More fancifully, even his curious triangular cipher may have been a kind of secret Hebrew greeting, as Maurice David suggests.

Columbus may have chosen to mention Genoa only when it was clearly in his interest to do so, such as when he had to impress the Courts of Europe. A man from Genoa may have been able to gain a captive audience, because the city was known for its seafaring and map-making. Certainly, when he arrived at Lisbon, he was known as a 'stranger', Colombo from Genoa. He came equipped with considerable seafaring experience, gained between bouts of work in his father's inn and at the loom. Columbus had needed to write nothing during these years, and consequently when he learnt to write we should not be surprised that his language was a strange blend of Genoese dialect, Portuguese and Spanish - the route his travels had taken him until then. The suggestion that he studied at the University of Pavia, as stated by his nineteenth century biographer Washington Irving, is almost certainly an invention of his son Ferdinand.

At the end of the day we ought perhaps to let Columbus himself speak. In 1502, in a letter he wrote to the directors of the Bank of San Giorgio, Genoa, he remarks at one point that 'although my body wanders here, my heart is continually at Genoa'. More directly still, in the bequests he makes to his son, he tellingly reaffirms 'since from Genoa I came and therein was I born'.

Christopher Columbus

Chapter III

The Women in his Life

Columbus never mentions his mother, Susanna Fontanarossa, by name, perhaps, as we have suggested, because he wished to hide his humble origins in the backstreets of Genoa. She reared five children. Apart from Christopher, who was the oldest, there was Giovanni Pellegrino, who died prematurely; Bartholomew, who went into partnership with Christopher as a map-maker in Lisbon; Giacomo (Diego); and a daughter, Bianchetta. Supporting such a large family was made more difficult when the family weaving business failed, and they were forced to move across Genoa to a smaller house. Unfortunately Domenico was a poor businessman, and in 1470 he was arrested for debt. Susanna, on the other hand, seems to have been much more practical and to have acquired money, for after a short stay in nearby Savona she returned to Genoa where, in 1477, she bought a better house, this time with a garden, in the Sant'Andrea quarter. By now Columbus had been sailing for a number of years as a merchant mariner. His mother's determination to surmount obstacles, and her perseverance in the face of difficulties made an impact on the young Columbus and served him well in his own relentless struggle to realise his ambitions.

Five other women whom he met in the years before 1492 had a significant influence on him. Above all, they listened sympathetically to his plans, keeping up his spirits, and when everything seemed to be going against him these same women offered him understanding and protection.

It was soon after he arrived in Lisbon in 1476 that he encountered the young Felipa Moniz Perestrello. The story goes that their eyes first met at mass in All Saints Convent. It was a less surprising venue than may appear at first because the chapel was open to the public and was renowned for matchmaking. Furthermore, the Convent was close to Columbus and Bartholomew's little map shop. Though Columbus was a mere chart-maker of lowly birth, and a foreigner at that, Felipa was fascinated by his arresting presence, and for her it was love at first sight. She was two or three years younger than Columbus - attractive, though not regarded as a beauty. By temperament she seems to have been rather timid and withdrawn, but her feelings for him were obviously strong enough to overcome any reservations about the suitability of the relationship.

The couple continued to meet at the Convent until, in the telling words of Columbus's son, Ferdinand, 'she became so familiar and friendly that she became his wife'. They were married at Lisbon in late 1479, or early 1480, on Columbus's return from his long voyage to Iceland and Ireland. Later that year, a son, Diego, was born. For Christopher, he was the issue of a calculated marriage which gave him a valuable link with two power-ful Portuguese families. Felipa was the daughter of a gentleman, Bartolomeo Perestrello, who had gained considerable seafaring experi-ence with Prince Henry the Navigator of Portugal and was hereditary captain of the island of Porto Santo in the Madeiras. When her father died, Felipa and her mother had left Porto Santo and come to live in Lisbon. Now with a reduced income, the mother must have been relieved at the prospect of her daughter's marriage with a man who asked for no dowry, and whose forceful personality encouraged her to believe that he would not remain a humble sea captain all his life.

Once married, the couple went out to live in Porto Santo where, much to Columbus's advantage, Felipa continued to have influence in the gov-ernment. More important still, the relationship gave him access to her father's maps and pilot-books (Portolans) on ocean navigation. In their brief five-year marriage Columbus showed no evidence of any deep love towards her. He used and deceived her, and when she died in 1485 he did not show much grief.

Before her death he had already met Beatrice de Moya, one of three Beatrices who were to enter his life. Born Beatrice Hernandez de Bobadilla, on her marriage to Andrea de Cabrera she became the Marquise de Moya. This did not prevent her from being fascinated by Columbus, above all by his determination, and there followed a passion-ate affair. More important from Columbus's point of view, she was a close friend of Queen Isabella, and Columbus used this special relation-ship to gain an audience.

The second Beatrice was Beatrice, la Enríquez de Harana. A young girl fifteen years his junior, she first caught his eye at Córdoba in late 1485. He was there, as usual, on business. On this occasion the business was to interest Isabella and Ferdinand in his great project. There are sev-eral stories about Beatrice's origins. One says that she was of humble birth, and that when Columbus met her she was serving in an inn; another that she came from a long-established noble Córdoban family. The latter sounds more likely. Columbus always had an eye for powerful contacts and the advantages they might bring in gaining an audience at court. Recent research, however, shows beyond doubt that she was an orphan of peasant birth, living with her late mother's cousin, Rodrigo, an unusually well-educated wine presser. So began a love affair, culminating in August 1488 with the birth of a bastard son, Ferdinand, who was later to write a biography of his father. Though a free man since his wife's death, Columbus did not marry Beatrice Enríquez, for he could gain no advan-tage from the match. Indeed, after the first voyage, they probably ceased living together; nor was she present at his deathbed. The affair left its mark on Columbus, nevertheless, and he felt a sense of responsibility for her for the rest of his life. In 1502 he ordered his son Diego to pay Beatrice the ten thousand maravedís he had been given as a reward for being the first to sight land in October 1492. Shortly afterwards, as he was about to leave on his fourth voyage, he wrote to Diego once again to 'take care of Beatrice Enríquez, for the love of me, as much as you would of your Mother', and he repeated the request in his will.

The third Beatrice in Columbus's life was Beatrice de Peraza y Bobadilla who came from an illustrious family, being the first cousin once removed of the Marquise de Moya. Brought up in the Canaries, she spent her infancy and some of her adolescence with the future Queen Isabella at a convent in Avila and as a maid of honour at Court. For a time, when she was seventeen, Beatrice became King Ferdinand of Aragon's mistress. Queen Isabella hoped to put an end to this liaison by marrying her off to Hernan Peraza. When her husband died in November 1488, Beatrice became an eligible widow of less than thirty. Vivacious and beautiful, by all accounts, Columbus quickly fell under her spell. When he returned home from his first voyage in 1493 marriage may have crossed his mind, but if it did, it was soon shelved in favour of a second expedition.

Columbus's ultimate objective had always been to win the support of the most powerful woman in the land, the Queen herself, and he had used his affairs with the three Beatrices to gain admission to her Court. Columbus and Isabella were about the same age. She was striking in appearance - with bright blue eyes, glowing chestnut hair and a fresh complexion. He made an impact on her from the moment of their first meeting. Above all she respected him : whereas others mocked, and her husband was cool towards his ideas, Isabella was at first intrigued and then enthusiastic about his plans and encouraged him greatly. Deeply devout herself, she had enough imagination and vision to believe in his ambitious project to spread Christianity round the world. Although she would not reach a decision without consulting her advisers, her great skills of diplomacy and tact meant that she always treated Columbus with dignity during his tortuous period of waiting. The story of her offering to pawn her own jewels to help finance the expedition is sheer myth, but she certainly aided Columbus by providing him with the ships he needed for his voyage and continued to befriend him throughout his varying fortunes.

Every woman in Columbus's life had a role to play. His mother's business efficiency and sheer determination was an early source of inspiration. His wife, Felipa, gave him access to powerful families and to her father's nautical library when he was young; she also provided him with a son and heir. The three Beatrices offered him comfort during his years of agonising wait, and, as far as they were able to, strengthened his influence at Court. An audience here was of supreme importance because, of all the women he met, it was to be Queen Isabella herself who was to play the most practical part in helping him realise his great ambition.

11. Queen Isabella by an unknown artist [Windsor Castle]

Chapter IV

God or Gold :
Religious Crusader or Merchant Adventurer?

What of Columbus the man? As we have noted, most contemporaries agree that he had striking looks. He was of above average height, with a long, noble face. This impressive appearance undoubtedly did much to command respect and admiration, and helped to generate an air of authority. Without it he would not have achieved that all-important hearing in the courts first of Portugal and then of Spain. Nor, later, would he have succeeded in preventing his terrified crew from overpowering him.

The overriding personal quality that his contemporaries remarked on was his unlimited imagination. His vision gave him the strength to grapple with any obstacle that stood in the way of his ambitious dream: to take the Gospel to the Indies. Calculating and enterprising, purposeful and resourceful, he knew exactly what he wanted from life, and he was confident that he would achieve it, no matter how difficult it was to be. The hardship and poverty he had endured as a boy in Genoa only made him more resilient. In the last analysis they also add to the magnitude of his achievement.

Columbus had enormous reserves of energy. He drove himself hard and was able to withstand fatigue. He often went without sleep. His daring and courage were also vital qualities in a mental world rife with fantastic tales - of seas full of demons and of lands inhabited by cannibals. In the words of a biographer, he possessed 'that spirit which enables one to encounter dangers without fear' [Thacher (1903-4) p.165]. His faith kindled a fire within him, and the flames leapt enthusiastically. Only occasionally do we sense a flicker - a doubt that his dream may, after all, be shattered. Everything took second place to the relentless pursuit of his obsession. There was no place in his life for enjoyment, and his personal habits were modest, even puritanical.

Columbus was a difficult man to communicate with. He was a deeply contemplative person, with no real ties of friendship. Most of the time he was moody, silent, even mystical, like a prophet committed to his defined task in life. He was suspicious of the motives of others, almost to the point of paranoia. Furtive and secret himself, there seems to have been little, if any, real happiness in his life. He trusted nobody apart from his family - about whom he says so little and stands out as a melancholy figure, with no sense of humour. He was an egotist, hardly aware of others;

It was he who had been chosen, and this gave him a special feeling of importance.

He did not find human relationships easy. Though usually self controlled, he could be angry when crossed. His unwillingness to share power with anyone led to frequent quarrels with his captains, especially with Martín Alonso Pinzón, whom he regarded as little short of a traitor. In handling his men he displayed much less firmness and lacked the confidence he showed when making practical decisions. This weakness posed serious difficulties ashore where he failed to command sufficient respect to administer the lands of which he had taken possession.

It is only to be expected that writers in a secular age such as ours should play down the significance of the religious dimension of Columbus's voyages in favour of a more materialistic interpretation. According to some commentators, Columbus's own claims to be a man with a divine mission cannot be taken at face value. They argue that he was less motivated by the desire to convert souls than by personal ambition, greed and the excitement and adventure conjured up by an uncharted sea. Do these comments stand up to investigation?

To be sure, the conditions which Columbus set the King and Queen of Spain before setting off on his first voyage show all the signs of megalomaniac self-interest. One was that he should be ennobled and called Don. Another was that he should receive the titles of Chief Admiral of the Ocean Sea and Perpetual Viceroy and Governor of all the islands and continents conquered. He even demanded a one tenth share of all profits accruing to Spain.

Furthermore in his Log Book he concentrates longingly on the lure of gold, pearls and spices awaiting him in Cipangu [Japan], Cathay [China] and the Indies. The notes he made in the margin of d'Ailly's great geography book, which he took with him, reinforce the idea that he was fascinated to the point of obsession with material things and took relatively little aesthetic interest in his surroundings.

Evidence of this kind has led some writers to conclude that Columbus was nothing more than a mean, avaricious, merchant adventurer who, far from deserving heroic status, deserves only our contempt. This, to my mind, is a great mistake, and does him a grave injustice.

The religious side of Columbus's character has received far too little attention, partly because of the later enslavement of people in the lands he discovered. This is quite unfair. Columbus cannot be held responsible for the actions of his successors. We must look instead at what the man himself did, and what he said.

Beyond all doubt Columbus was a deeply religious man. He fasted strictly, and confessed and took Communion regularly. He prayed at canonical hours, and throughout his life remained deeply attached to the Franciscan Order. He was especially fascinated by the Old Testament, and quotes chapter and verse from it to support his actions. He sincerely believed that the success of his first voyage to the Indies had nothing to do with reason, mathematics or maps: 'it was but a fulfilment of what had been foretold by the prophet Isaiah'. God would give him victory over apparent impossibilities. He would always guide and protect him. This meant that nothing in his life happened by chance: it was all down to Providence. He noted how God had recently secured the peaceful union of the kingdoms of Castile and Aragon. It seemed that he had a special interest in the well-being of Spain; and He would therefore tend to the welfare of Columbus, who sailed from its shores and in its name.

God had given him a mission in life: 'Our Almighty God has shown me the highest favour which, since David, he has not shown to anybody'. As the predestined agent of God, his brief was to champion the Christian religion overseas and, in the longer term, to restore Jerusalem to the Christian world. To this end, he made Queen Isabella promise that she would spend all the wealth gained by the Crown in financing armies to win back Jerusalem. The complete assurance he had in his objective might almost be mistaken for vanity. To him alone had God entrusted this great mission; consequently only he could succeed. Earlier projects had been destined to fail precisely because God had willed that they should. This time, however, it would be different, for Columbus could legitimately introduce himself to the natives as a representative of God:

> ...we shall endeavour to turn all these peoples into Christians... Christendom shall make good business with them... for this was the end and the beginning of the enterprise, that it should lead to the increase and glory of the Christian religion...

Columbus's lust for gold must be seen in this context. It was not primarily for personal gain but to finance a holy war, in which he would rescue Jerusalem from 'the infidel' and go on to meet the so-called Grand Khan, the High King of the East. As he explains in the *Prologue to the Journal of his First Voyage,* the Grand Khan 'had sent to Rome many times to ask for learned men of our holy faith to teach him'. He now called upon the Catholic sovereigns, as they loved the Christian faith and were great enemies of the sect of Mahomet, to send him to the princes of India 'with a view that they might be converted to our holy faith'. The emphasis here is squarely on the missionary motive: the prospect of saving souls. He says nothing about searching for a route to the Indies for economic reasons. Nor, interestingly enough, does he mention making new discoveries *en route.*

In this respect Columbus saw himself as a second St Christopher. In the third century St Christopher is supposed to have learnt about Christianity from a hermit while living on the banks of a river and then spent his time helping travellers across the river. One day, according to the tale, a child asked Christopher to help him across. Christopher found

12. The Grand Khan, or High King of the East
    [from J. Mandeville *Libro de las meravillas del mundo* (1524 edn)]

[Unknown to Columbus, the last Grand Khan Prester John, had died more
than two centuries earlier.]

the child unexpectedly heavy, and the child confided to him that he was
in reality Jesus and that Christopher was therefore carrying the weight of
the world on his shoulders. Columbus was very much aware of this legend, which had spread to the west during the ninth century and had
appeared in the *Golden Legend* in the twelfth. He had almost certainly
seen it depicted in one of the countless works which it inspired all over
Europe.

Columbus resembled St Christopher in a number of ways. He was tall,
with great physical and mental strength; he, too, had a fearful appearance.
His christian name, 'Cristoferens' - the bearer of Christ - was especially
appropriate. Just as the legendary St Christopher had borne travellers
across the river, so Columbus also would 'bear' Christ. He would bear
him 'on his shoulders by conveying and leading' (Columbus the sailor;
the man of enterprise); 'in his body, by making it lean' (by fasting); 'and
in his mind by devotion'. Finally he would bear Christ in his mouth:
through confession and preaching, he would help bring the Catholic faith
to souls awaiting him in islands at the other side of the ocean.

His ultimate purpose was a new crusade to recover the Holy
Sepulchre, seized by the Turks at the capture of Jerusalem in 1077. After
early successes and much suffering and sacrifice, the crusades of the

twelfth and thirteenth centuries had ended in failure and exhausted the treasuries of Europe. The Holy Sepulchre, or tomb, in which Jesus was supposed to have lain for three days before his resurrection, was still in the hands of the Moslems.

Columbus was continuing the work of the crusades. This was his mission in life. We can only fully understand him if we keep this visionary project at the forefront of our attention when we trace the events of his life. Of course, fame, riches and the search for adventure entered into it, and undoubtedly became more important as Columbus realised the economic possibilities of his discovery - it would be absurd to pretend they did not - but they were always secondary to his overriding religious objective.

Christopher Columbus

Chapter V

The First Voyage, 1492-3 :
Victory over the Impossible

'All seas are navigable... àll seas are peopled by lands'.

Such were Columbus's comments scribbled in the margin of his copy of *Imago Mundi*. Whenever he was not at sea, he could immerse himself in geography books and pore over maps, for his brother Bartholomew had a shop in Lisbon where Christopher had been living since at least 1476.

His seafaring experience now widened with voyages to Thule (Iceland), Ireland and possibly Bristol. In 1477 he moved with Felipa to Madeira. While there, working partly as a sailor, partly as a merchant, he is said to have witnessed a terrible storm, during which a sailing vessel was washed up at Porto Santo. All but the helmsman had died during the storm, and Columbus offered this ailing man hospitality in his house. A man whose head was already full of tales of islands seen in the distance and of unusually carved pieces of wood, now became party to the sailor's great secret. He is supposed to have told him that on the other side of the ocean there was land waiting to be discovered, and proceded to produce a map for Columbus to show where it lay. Even if this story is true, which I doubt, he had to wait another ten years before he could investigate the sailor's claim.

It was not until after he returned from an expedition to Guinea in 1483 that he succeeded in obtaining an audience with King John II of Portugal. At this stage Columbus had no comprehensive plan. He proposed to go to India and Japan, and to China to meet the Grand Khan. Gold, silver and pearls also featured in the plan. To execute it, he demanded the status and privileges of an Admiral of Castile. John rejected the plan late in 1484.

Undeterred, Columbus moved to Spain and, between 1486 and 1492, negotiated relentlessly with those in power. He approached the itinerant Spanish court first in Seville and subsequently in Córdoba and Granada. Failing to interest the Duke of Medina-Sidonia, he applied to the Duke of Medinaceli, who though much readier to listen, decided to devote his energies to war against the Moors.

In January 1486 Columbus approached Alonso de Quintanilla, the Chief Treasurer and Accountant of Ferdinand and Isabela, and gained a hearing before the Cardinal of Spain, Mendoza. That Spring, he had his first interview with the King and Queen at Córdoba. They listened attentively as he talked excitedly through his plans; in his hand he held Toscanelli's map full of fabulous islands. They realised that they were not competent to judge the question, and it was clear in any case that the project could not be commissioned while Spain was still embroiled in a war against the Moors. They sent him to a committee of experts, chaired by Fray Hernando de Talavera. Talavera was unsympathetic to Columbus from the start. He felt ill at ease in his company, and was even less impressed when Columbus proceded to outline his project without producing a realistic map. Eventually, in 1490, the Commisssion presented an unfavourable report.

Believing his quest was a lost cause, Columbus set off for the monastery of La Rábida where his eleven-year-old son Diego was staying. Here he met Fray Juan Pérez, who wrote the King and Queen a letter of support. He also met the astrologer Antonio de Marchena, who was held in high esteem by Ferdinand and Isabella, and Martín Alonso Pinzón of Palos, an established sea-captain, who was thirsty for further adventure.

In the short term the meeting with Pérez was the more significant. It gained Columbus a second audience at Court. This was the occasion on which he laid down his conditions: that he should be knighted and assume the title of Don; that his status be raised to that of Grand Admiral, Viceroy and Perpetual Governor of any lands he discovered; and that he should receive a ten per cent cut in the subsequent profits accruing from these lands. The extravagance of these demands led to a second dismissal from Court. As he left, he toyed with the idea of presenting his project to France or England.

On that same day his friend Luis de Santángel, Minister of Finance, intervened, pleading with Ferdinand and Isabella, who had accepted his plan in principle, not to haggle over the exact conditions. The Queen relented and despatched a messenger, who caught up with Columbus at the Bridge of Pinos and persuaded him to return. As fortune had it, in January 1492 Granada had fallen to the Spanish. The final stumbling block had been removed: the monarchs' hands were free, and the way was now open for Columbus.

What follows is a reconstruction of the log he kept during this momentous voyage. It is partly based on the evidence of Bartholomé de Las Casas and that of Columbus's son, Ferdinand:

Saturday, 12 May 1492

I left the city of Granada and came to the town of Palos, which is a seaport used to providing the King and Queen with ships. Here I equipped three vessels well suited for my voyage. Their names were the *Santa María*, my own ship; the *Pinta* whose captain was Martín Alonso Pinzón; and the *Niña* which was commanded by his brother, Vicente Yáñez Pinzón of Palos.

13. Columbus leaving the King and Queen on the shore of Spain by Theodor de Bry (1590)

Friday, 3 August

We set sail for the Canaries half an hour before sunrise. There were ninety men on board. A strong breeze was felt all that day until sunset. I intend to keep a journal during my voyage and will note down all that I see and the distances travelled each day.

Monday, 6 August

The rudder of the *Pinta* jumped its gudgeons and the crew had to use sails. I joined the ship as fast as I could, suspecting foul play by its owner, Cristóbal Quintero, who I already knew had reservations about the voyage. Pinzón secured the rudder with rope.

Tuesday, 7 August

A gust of wind snapped the rope and further repairs were needed. Once these were made, we continued in the direction of Lanzarote in the Canaries.

Wednesday, 8 August

The *Pinta* was still steering badly, and letting in water. She really needs replacing.

Thursday, 9 August

We sighted the Canaries at dawn. I told Pinzón to find another ship to replace the damaged one. In the meantime, the *Santa María* and the *Niña* made for the island of Gomera. Here, alas, our landing was delayed for two days, due to a mixture of unfavourable winds and calms.

Sunday, 12 August

My hopes of obtaining a replacement ship from Doña Beatriz de Bobadilla, the mistress of the island, fell through. The men were greatly annoyed at this; but I believe it was God's will. Therefore, I ordered that the *Pinta's* rudder be repaired at the next opportunity.

Thursday, 23 August

We passed the night near Tenerife. How astonished the crew were to see huge flames issuing from the volcano there.

Saturday, 25 August

After a difficult passage, I reached the Grand Canary, Pinzón having arrived the day before. Here the *Pinta's* rudder was replaced. The *Niña's* latteen sails were substituted for square ones. This will enable her to follow the other two ships more easily and safely.

Friday, 31 August

Now fully repaired, the ships set out from the Grand Canary.

Sunday, 2 September

I returned to Gomera. Here we spent four days loading on meat, wood and water. I was heartened to hear that many of the people from these parts claimed to have seen land to the west of the Canaries.

Thursday, 6 September

We sailed west from Gomera. I can truly say that our ocean crossing began today. Progress was slow, on account of the winds being feeble and variable.

Friday, 7 September

We still lay between Gomera and Tenerife, our ships becalmed.

Saturday, 8 September

Water broke over our bows, slowing us down. I was not unduly perturbed by a report that three Portuguese caravels were intent on capturing us. No doubt the King of Portugal is seeking revenge for me turning to Spain to commission my expedition.

Sunday, 9 September

We completely lost sight of land, and the crew were worried lest they should never see it again. I reprimanded them for steering so badly, whilst at the same time encouraging them with promises of lands and riches. From this day onwards, I decided to record a shorter distance than we had actually covered. This was so that the men would not think they were so far away from Spain, and not be so anxious. I will, of course, keep a secret, accurate, reckoning of my own.

Monday, 10 September

Although we went sixty leagues today, I noted down only forty-eight, so that the crew might not be alarmed if the voyage should be long.

Tuesday, 11 September

Today we saw a large piece of mast decaying in the water, but could not get hold of it. At dusk, we were about one hundred and fifty leagues west of the island of Ferro.

Thursday, 13 September

The compass needles last night pointed, not to the north, but to another point slightly west. This morning, we found them slightly east of north.

Friday, 14 September

The men on board the *Niña* reported that they had seen a tern and a reedtail. These are the first birds we have seen on our voyage.

Saturday, 15 September

That night, a great flame fell from the heavens into the sea, close to where the ships were.

Sunday, 16 September

We were surprised to see the whole surface of the water covered with a great mass of yellowish green weed. It occurred to us that it may have come from a nearby island or reef. It has been a cloudy day, and there was a little rain. We noticed how the breezes were very temperate. The mornings particularly are most delightful. It reminds me of April in Andalusia. All that is missing is the song of nightingales.

Monday, 17 September

Today we saw even more weed, this time with stalks and shoots loaded with fruit. This was a clear indication that we were near land. I saw a live crab amid the weed and kept it. A little later I saw tunny fish. The men in the *Niña* killed a dolphin with a harpoon. Another tropic bird was sighted. This species is not accustomed to sleeping on the sea, and so was another sign of land. I trust in that High God, in whose hands are all victories, that very soon we shall indeed sight land.

Tuesday, 18 September

The sea was as smooth as a river. I drew close to Pinzón, who was ahead, to hear that a great flock of birds had been seen moving westward. I was confident of finding land that night. At dusk I saw a large cloud, which is usually a good guide to land being near. The crews wanted me to search to the north for land. This I refused to do because it disagreed with my calculations and would waste a lot of time. That night, having sailed for eleven days under full sail, we took in our top-sails because the wind had freshened.

Wednesday, 19 September

During the day, two pelicans flew over the ships. We sensed that land was near-by, but the weather being favourable I wanted to press on to the Indies rather than stop at mere islands. These could always be visited on the return voyage.

Thursday, 20 September

Three more pelicans flew over the ship. My men also caught a bird like a tern but more resembling a river bird. Later, three little birds flew over the ship. Surely these would not stray far from land. The weed in this area is so thickly matted that it held back the ships. Wherever possible, we tried to avoid it altogether.

Friday, 21 September

The weed was still extremely thick at dawn. Once again the sea was smooth. Progress was slow. We only travelled thirteen leagues that day and night because there was little wind. We sighted a whale which would not have ventured far from shore.

Saturday, 22 September

From time to time today we faced a contrary wind. This relieved some of the crew, for until now the wind has been behind us all the time which caused them to worry about how we should ever get back to Spain.

Sunday, 23 September

Even now, some continued to grumble, saying that the wind would never blow hard enough to get them back. At about nine in the morning we saw a pigeon, and in the afternoon we saw a pelican, a small river bird and some white birds, like gulls. These, I told my men, were clear signs that we were near land. Praise God that we have the same help in finding land as God gave to Moses when leading the Jews out of Egypt.

Monday, 24 Septenber

All further signs of land proved to be false alarms, and only had the effect of pro-voking fear and restlessness amongst the men. They have begun to meet together and have mocked what they describe as the Admiral's 'mad fantasy'. One of their schemes which I got wind of was to throw me overboard and report back in Spain that I had fallen into the sea accidentally while observing the stars. I threatened to punish all plotters severely, while trying to offset their fears by speaking of the imminent prospect of sighting land.

Tuesday, 25 September

While I was talking to Pinzón, who had come alongside the *Santa María*, he sud-denly cried out 'Land, land, sir!' I claim the reward'' He pointed to what seemed to be an island about twenty-five leagues away. The crew of the Niña climbed the mast and rigging, and confirmed that it was land. Everyone fell on their knees and thanked God. Myself, I was used to such misplaced hopes. Yet I didn't want to destroy their optimism because I wanted them to continue the voyage. I even steered in that direction most of the night.

Wednesday, 26 September

The crew were forced to accept that what had appeared to be land had simply been squall clouds. We continued to sail west on a calm sea. A pelican and some other birds were sighted.

Saturday, 29 September

Our progress was delayed by calms. We saw a frigate-bird. These birds have the extraordinary habit of pursuing pelicans until, out of fright, they vomit up what they have just eaten. The frigate-birds then catch this undigested food in the air. These birds never go more than about twenty leagues from land. After dinner, we saw a lot of weed, three more pelicans and another frigate-bird.

Sunday, 30 September

Four birds flew together over the ship, a sign that land was near. Below, some rather exotic emperor fish, with hard skins, were noticed. That night I continued to let the stars be my guide, but calms once again made our going slow.

Monday, 1 October

There was a great rain storm. Today I recorded in the log that we had travelled five hundred and eighty leagues from Ferro. Secretly, I recorded the true figure of seven hundred and seven leagues.

Tuesday, 2 October

We saw many fish and caught a small tunny. A white bird like a sea gull was spotted, and many other birds besides. The sea remained smooth and calm. It carried a powdery seaweed.

Wednesday, 3 October

Fewer birds were seen today. this made the men anxious that they had accidentally passed between some islands. I refused to look for these islands because I feared losing a favourable wind. I also felt that I should lose my men's confidence if I sailed aimlessly to look for islands. Far from having the desired effect, it caused the men to start plotting against me once again.

Thursday, 4 October

God was pleased to assist me with new signs of land today. In all, we saw more than forty petrels. Two pelicans also flew by, one so close that a boy was able to hit it with a stone.

Saturday, 6 October

Pinzón wanted to set a course for Cipangu. I thought this unwise, believing that
we must lose no time in finding the mainland of the Indies : the islands could
wait.

Sunday, 7 October

At dawn it really did seem this time that there was land lying to the west.
Nobody, of course, dared to announce this for fear of losing the reward offered by
the King and Queen. The ships sailed on as fast as they could. Suddenly, the
Niña, which had been sailing ahead, fired a gun and hoisted her flags to indicate
that she had sighted land. Even now, it proved to be an illusion, and land was not
seen again.

Yet, God saw to it that we were offered more signs. We saw many large flocks of
birds coming from the west and flying southwest in search of food. Surely, these
small birds would not fly far from land. Recalling that the Portuguese had made
most of their discoveries by noting the flights of birds, I steered west by south-
west. But it was in this direction that I expected to find Cipangu in any case.

Monday, 8 October

Thanks be to God, the air is very soft like April in Seville. It is a pleasure to be
here, so balmy are the breezes. The sea, too, is just like the river at Seville. A
dozen highly-coloured field birds came to the ship.

Wednesday, 10 October

Birds passed overhead during the night and day. Alas, this sign did nothing to sat-
isfy the men, whose desire to reach land had got to fever pitch. I told the men that
they *had to* go through with the enterprise. If they had faith they would soon discover land.

Thursday, 11 October

Today we came across the roughest seas of the voyage so far. Thankfully, God
gave us clear indications that we were near land. First, a green branch was sighted; and then a large green fish was found near reefs. The crew of the *Pinta* saw a
cane and a stick covered with barnacles. Soon after they fished up another stick
which was most skillfully carved, a small board, and a lot of weeds similar to
those found on shore. The *Niña's* crew saw a thorn branch loaded with red berries
that seemed to have been freshly cut. All the men rejoiced at these signs. That
evening, when they sang the usual Hail Mary, I told them that God had shown
them his favour by conducting them safely to land. Just this once, I permitted
night sailing but I urged the men to be extra watchful. The King and Queen of
Spain had promised ten thousand maravedís per annum for the rest of their life to
the first person to sight land. On top of this, I personally now offered a silk dou-
blet.

At ten at night, I thought I saw light, like a small wax candle. As yet I was not
sure enough to risk announcing that it was land. I quickly summoned the King's

servant, Pedro Gutiérrez, who said he also saw it. After this, we saw the light intermittently. It seemed to be moving up and down. I thought perhaps it was the torch of fishermen or other travellers, moving from house to house.

Friday, 12 October

At about two in the morning, the swifter *Pinta,* which was far ahead, fired the signal for land. Some sailor by the name of Rodrigo de Triana claimed that he had first sighted it from a distance of about two leagues. But my claim to the reward was more proper because I had first seen the light more than four hours earlier. this was the spiritual light that was going to illuminate these parts of the world. Forthwith, we took in all but the mainsail. It seemed an endless wait until dawn, when, eventually we saw an island, about fifteen leagues long, very flat, full of green trees and much fruit. It abounded in springs and had a lake in the middle. This must indeed be the Indies!

14. *The Landing of Columbus,* 12 October 1492 *
   [As Columbus plants the flag of Spain, the brothers Pinzón hold other standards and a Franciscan friar bears a crucifix]

The astonished inhabitants rushed to the shore. They took the ships to be some kind of animals. We cast anchor, and then I went ashore in an armed boat, displaying the royal standard. The two Pinzóns did the same, holding high the banner of Ferdinand and Isabella with its green cross and crowns.

---

* Strictly speaking the landing was on 21 October 1492 in our modern way of reckoning. Surprisingly, the date of this momentous event was never altered when the Gregorian Calendar replaced the Julian Calendar in 1582.

The men knelt on the ground and kissed the earth in thanks to God. Upon rising, I formally took possession of the island in the name of the Catholic Sovereigns, giving it the name of San Salvador, the blessed Saviour. We learnt later that the Indians call it Guanahaní [*there is still great debate today as to whether it was Watling Island or Samaná* Cay]. The mood of my men had changed : they were now swearing obedience to me, and begging forgiveness for showing so little faith during the voyage.

I quickly formed the impression that the Indians, who watched all this celebrating, were a gentle, peaceful people. I knew that they would be more easily converted to Christianity by love than by force. With this in mind, I gave some of them red caps, glass beads and bells for sparrow hawks. All of these trifles they cherished, as if they were precious stones. Some swam out to our ships; others paddled out in their canoes. Until dusk, they brought us parrots, cotton and darts in exchange. It appeared to me that they were a poor people.

They go around as naked as when their mothers bore them, women as well as men. Not one I saw was over thirty years old. Their bodies were well formed, they had broad brows, straight legs and no bellies. Their hair was as coarse as a horse's tail. In most cases it was cut above the ears but some had let it grow down to their shoulders, and had it tied about their heads with a strong cord. Their skins were olive-coloured, making them look like the Canary Islanders. Some paint themselves black, others white, and still others red. Some painted just their face, others painted the whole body; some painted around the eyes, others painted the nose. They know little about weapons because when I showed them swords they took them by the blade and cut themselves. All they have to defend themselves with are pointed darts. Some of them had scars on their bodies which seem to have been caused by attackers from adjacent islands.

They should make good, intelligent servants. I also believe that they could be made good Christians, as they seem to have no religion at the moment. When I leave, I shall take six of them back to Spain with me so that they can learn to speak.

Saturday, 13 October

At daybreak, many Indians came to the beach and used something like bakers' shovels to paddle their canoes out to our ships. Their canoes are lightweight and skillfully made; they are of varying size, capable of holding from one person up to forty-five. All day the bartering continued. They seemed happy even to take away pieces of broken crockery, parts of a glazed bowl and pieces of broken glass. Some gave as much as four hundred pounds of cotton for just three Portuguese coins. They were sure that they were buying souvenirs from heaven. The only jewels or metal objects they had were some gold pendants worn through a hole in the nostrils. They signified that the gold came from the south where there lived a king who had many tiles and vessels of gold; but they would not take us there. They added that all around them were many other islands and large countries. I intend to lose no more time and shall be setting off soon in a south-westerly direction for the great island of Cipangu.

Sunday, 14 October

We sailed along the coast in a north-easterly direction. The natives ran along the shore as we went by, offering us food and water. They lay down and raised their hands in thanks, and then called to others to see us, the men who had come from heaven. Some invited us to come ashore to rest. I gave them glass beads and pins but decided not to land due to a great reef of rocks. On the other side of the island, I found a great harbour, capable of holding all the ships in the Christian world. Eventually, we came to a peninsula which seemed to afford an excellent site for a fort. I saw six huts with gardens as beautiful as those of Castile in April and May but the land did not hold much promise of riches.

We sailed off to one of the hundred or more neighbouring islands, taking with us seven Indians to learn how to speak and to act as guides. If your Highnesses wish, I could take all the inhabitants of the island back to Castile. If they prefer it, we could hold them as slaves on the island. Fifty men would do the trick, they are very unskilled in arms.

Monday, 15 October

My desire was not to pass any island without taking possession but there were so many that I did not know which one to go to first. At midday I approached the nearest and largest of these islands, which I named Santa María de la Concepción [Rum Kay] out of devotion to the Virgin Mary. It was almost dusk when I dropped anchor at the western end of the island. That night one of the Indians we had captured in San Salvador swam to the shore and fled.

Tuesday, 16 October

I went ashore in an armed boat to see if there really was as much gold as the captive Indians claimed. A large canoe came alongside the *Niña* and another of the Indians jumped into it and succeeded in escaping. Shortly afterwards, another canoe came up to the ship. The man in it wanted to barter cotton but because he would not leave his vessel the crew seized him. Seeing all this from the poop of my ship, I sent for the man and gave him gifts, among which were small bells which I placed in his ears. I hoped this would create a good impression on him and make a second expedition easier for us.

At about midday, we sailed for the much larger island in the west. This I named Fernandina [Long Island] in honour of the King of Spain. Here, the natives are supposed to wear gold bracelets on their arms and legs, in their ears and nose, and around their neck.

On our way we picked up a man in a small canoe who was crossing from one island to another. He was carrying a piece of bread, a flask of water, some earth used by the Indians to paint their bodies, and some fragrant dried leaves. He also carried a string of green glass beads and two *blancas* in a little basket. From these coins, I deduced that he had originally come from San Salvador, and was going to spread news of the coming of the Christians throughout the islands.

I navigated all day with light winds. As we neared Fernandina it appeared very flat, green and fertile. Its beaches seemed free from rocks but had submerged reefs. On account of this, I decided not to drop anchor until the next morning. That night, we gave the Indian from the canoe bread, honey, something to drink, and some bits and pieces to distribute to the inhabitants of the island. He then went and gave such a good account of us that a huge number of natives came in their canoes, offering us water and bartering most intelligently. In return, we gave them glass beads, brass clappers and leather tags.

Fernandina far surpassed the other islands. It was bigger and more beautiful, with its streams and lakes. Not only did it abound in springs, trees and meadows but it had mountains and hills which the others lacked.

On this island I saw trees growing naturally with a single trunk but with four or five different kinds of leaves and branches, one resembling cane, another mastic. There were also some unusually shaped and brightly coloured fish. The only animals we saw were lizards, parrots and the occasional snake (iguana) which was a great delicacy for the Indians on account of its very white, soft and tasty meat.

Wednesday, 17 October

I set off at noon on a north by north-west course around the island of Fernandina. The wind was more favourable, however, to head directly for the goldfield on the island of Saometo, wilch I have re-christened Isabella [now Crooked Island] in honour of the Queen of Spain. On the way I lay anchor in a wonderful harbour, which though shallow, was wide enough to berth a hundred ships. A group of men guided some of the crew to their village to collect water. Whilst they were gone, I had a chance to look around. This land is the best and most fertile that there is in the world. I walked among the trees which were the most beautiful I have ever seen, and as green as those of Andalusia in the month of May.

The men reported on their return that the village only had about a dozen huts in it, all shaped like tents. Inside they were clean but very bare apart from their strange beds which they called hammocks. Some of the inhabitants owned dogs which could not bark but could only grunt. They also encountered a man who wore a large piece of gold with letters on it in his nose. I was very angry that the men had not had the courage to bargain for it.

After the water had been taken on board, I set sail. The clouds were thick and heavy as we skirted the coast that evening. After midnight there was heavy rain which fell almost until dawn.

Friday, 19 October

We ran westwards along the coast of the island until we reached a cape which I named Cabo Hermoso [Beautiful]. This is the most delightful island I have come across, with its thick groves and gentle hills. Everything on all these coasts is so green and lovely that I do not know where to go first, and my eyes never weary of looking on such fine vegetation, so different from ours. Many trees and plants grow here which I think will be highly valued in Spain for dyes and medicinal spices. I am ashamed and saddened not to know all their names.

Tomorrow, I plan to go inland to meet the king who is supposed to have a lot of gold, although I don't really believe it. Nor do I want to get bogged down in a detailed examination of the island, for this would take more than fifty years. My main object is to find gold and spices in quantity and to return to Spain in April.

Sunday, 21 October

After breakfast I went ashore at Cabo del Isleo. I only found one house, and this was deserted, the occupants must have run away in fright, leaving all their belongings behind. I forbade my men to touch any of these things. I then set out to explore the island. It is even more beautiful and green than the other islands. The vegetation is like that of Andalusia in April, and the small birds sing so sweetly that I would like to stay here for ever.

By the side of a lagoon I saw a snake. After a struggle we killed it, and I am bringing its skin home to show your Highnesses. Nearby, I came across aloe which I am told is very valuable. Tomorrow I shall see that half a ton of it is loaded on board.

I gave the natives small glass beads and bells for the feet of sparrow hawks, in exchange for fresh water. I am keen to see the king, so as to learn whether he really does have gold. After that, I shall head for the much larger island of Cipangu which the Indians call Colba [Cuba] and rate very highly. When I reach the city of the Grand Khan I shall deliver your Highnesses' letters.

Tuesday, 23 October

I am not prepared to spend any more time on this island waiting for the king and his gold. Unfortunately I could not sail for Colba today because there was no wind.

Wednesday, 24 October

At midnight I left Cape Isleo, bound for Colba where I hope to find gold, spices and other merchandise. From the globes and maps I have seen, Cipangu [Japan] cannot be far off.

Sunday, 28 October

Leaving Isabella on Wednesday, my progress was greatly impeded by strong winds. Laying anchor for a while at the Islas de Arena, I reached today what I believe to be the northern coast of Colba. Whether it is an island or not I cannot be sure. If it is an island, it would appear to be larger than England and Scotland put together. It is full of very beautiful high mountains, like in Sicily. I renamed the land Juana, after the heir to the throne of Castile.

I anchored in a very beautiful large river, edged by tall trees and surrounded by strange fruit and flowers. I recognised only wheat and purslane. Nearby, I came to two fishermens' huts but found that the people had fled, leaving their nets and tackle behind. In one hut there was another of those dogs which do not bark. I ordered my men not to touch anything.

Returning to the boat, I went up the river which I named San Salvador. The Indians from Guanahaní indicated that this was one of ten great rivers and that large ships belonging to the Grand Khan moor there.

Monday, 29 October

Today I saw another river, much larger than the others. I called it Río de Mares. Here I laid anchor. Thinking that a full-scale landing force would only scare the natives, I decided to send just two boats ashore, in one of which was an Indian. Even now, men, women and children all fled. Their houses, which more resembled tents, were rather haphazardly arranged but better than I had ever seen before, being skillfully constructed from palm branches. Inside were images of women and beautifully carved masks. Outside we found some skulls that were shaped like those of cows.

The songs of the birds and the chirping of crickets throughout the night lulled everyone to sleep. The air was soft and healthy, and it was neither hot nor cold.

Tuesday, 30 October

Leaving the Río de Mares, I steered north-west and came to a cape full of palm trees. I was uncertain whether this was Colba or not, not knowing whether Colba was a city on an island, or on a great continent stretching to the north. I decided to send the letter from the Spanish Sovereigns to the king of these parts, who I was told was at war with the Grand Khan. After that I must endeavour to reach the Grand Khan himself who would be either here or in Cathay.

Sunday, 4 November

Although the Indians of this region could not be more gentle and timid, I was told that a fair distance away there are monstrous men with one eye and others with dogs' noses. These men behead their enemies, castrate them and then drink their blood.

Monday, 5 November

The ships were brought on shore this morning, and one by one repaired and caulked. In the meantime we collected mastic to take home with us. Two men, who I had sent to explore the interior with two Indians, returned tonight and reported that they had reached a village containing fifty large tent-shaped huts, thatched with palm. The village leaders, who they noticed had lighter coloured skins than the Canarians, had carried them to the largest house and offered them roots to eat. The chairs they sat in were most extraordinary, being shaped like a short legged animal with a very broad tail. They had heads to them, with eyes and ears made of gold. These were obviously kept for special guests. The Indians sat around them and then, one by one, kissed the mens' hands and feet, believing them to have come from heaven. The males left and the women were brought in and did the same. They hoped my men were going to stay for at least five days.

All of the inhabitants had wanted to accompany the men to the ships for their return - to heaven - but only the king, his son and one servant were allowed to do so. On the way they passed many huts full of woven cotton which they used for making hammocks and cloth to cover the womens' private parts. Some of this cotton they later brought in baskets full to the ship, asking only for leather thongs in return. The two men also met many people, both men and women, who carried in their hands a half-burnt leaf containing herbs. This, apparently, they are used to sucking and drawing in its smoke with their breath.

Sunday, 11 November

A canoe came alongside the ship, with six youths in it. Five came aboard, and I ordered that they be detained. Later on, I sent to a house on the western side of the river and captured seven head of women, young ones and adults, and three small children. I did this because I believed that the men would be more content in Spain if they had women from their own land. That night, one of the women's husbands, who was the father of the three children on board, came alongside us in a canoe and pleaded with me to let him come too. They are all now happily reunited.

It seemed a good idea to take some captives from this area, so that they would have a chance to learn our language and tell us more about these lands. It is a wonderful thing that these people know nothing about theft or murder, and yet they have no religion. I am confident that when they return to their native country they will be able to help the Christian faith to spread.

Monday, 12 November

I set sail before dawn for the island of Bohío. The Indians told me that here people gather gold on the beach at night with candles, and go away to hammer it down into bars.

Friday, 16 November

Reaching an island in the Mar de Nuestra Señora, I made a cross out of two very large trees. There is sufficient depth in this port for the largest carrack in the world to anchor. A fortress could also be built here at little cost.

Meanwhile, the Indians on board the ship had found a great deal of mother-of-pearl. In one of their nets they caught a fish which looked just like a pig, except that it was covered with a very hard skin and had a soft tail. I ordered my men to salt it, so that it can be brought home for your Majesties to see.

Wednesday, 21 November

Lured away by the prospect of gold on Bohío, Martín Alonso Pinzón had the audacity to desert me today. There was no excuse whatsoever for his conduct. It was an act of gross disobedience and sheer greed on his part. I have come to expect such disloyal things from this man.

Thursday, 22 November

Tonight I shone a lantern out to Pinzón who had every opportunity of joining me if he had so chosen, but he did not.

Friday, 23 November

I can now see the large island of Bohío in the distance. The Indians say it is inhabited by ferocious cannibals and terrifying men who have one eye in their foreheads.

Saturday, 24 November

I anchored in a haven formed by a flat island [Cayo de Moa] and another island. This spot, which I have named Santa Caterina, could hold all the ships of Spain safe from the wind.

Sunday, 25 November

As we were taking on water from a river, I saw traces of gold in some stones. I ordered that some of these stones be collected and brought back to your Highnesses. Up on the hillsides, the pine trees stood so tall that they seemed almost to touch the sky; and we seized the opportunity to obtain a new mizzen mast for the *Niña*. This place of indescribable beauty also offers excellent prospects for development, for the strength of the river is sufficient to drive sawmills.

Tuesday, 27 November

I steered south-east down the coastline, and was charmed by the beauty and luxuriant foliage of the region. I was especially taken by the multitude of palm trees, the tallest and most beautiful specimens I have ever seen. The little birds and the verdure of the fields tempted me to stay there forever. This country is of such marvellous beauty that it surpasses all others. In spite of my best efforts to give your Highnesses a perfect account of it, my tongue could never tell the whole truth, nor my pen fully describe it. Above all, there is a very large population here which could be converted into good Catholics, to the glory of the Christian religion.

Thursday, 29 November

On the road today, my men came across an old man who was unable to run away. They caught him and gave him presents before letting him go. I wish they had brought the man to me as I would like to have spoken to him. In one of the huts, other men found a man's skull in a basket hanging from a post. Later on, the same thing was found in another village. I presumed it to be the skull of an ancestor but was unable to ask the Indians because they had fled.

Friday, 30 November

I sent eight well-armed men, accompanied by two of the Indians we have on board, to examine the villages inland and speak to the people. They came to many houses but found no one, all having run away. They saw four youths who were digging in the fields; but as soon as they saw my men, they also ran away at all speed.

Monday, 3 December

Today, one of the natives of this place made a long speech near the stern of the boat. I did not really understand what he said but I imagined that he was saying how pleased he was to see us. Suddenly, I noticed that an Indian on our ship, though a tall and strong man, had turned a shade of yellow and had started to tremble. Apparently, the natives intended to kill me. However, when we showed them one of our cross-bows and a sword, they all fled. We found them assembled a short way off, and I succeeded in exchanging copper ornaments, bells, glass beads and pieces of turtle-shell for their darts. Nearby, I saw a fine house, not very large but with two doors. Shells and many other objects were fastened to the ceiling and I thought that perhaps it was a temple. One of the inhabitants, who had now warmed towards us, climbed up and offered me anything that was there, and I gladly took some.

Wednesday, 5 December

After considerable delay on account of unfavourable winds, I finally set sail from the eastern end of Juana [Cuba]. Finding it imposslble to steer north-east to Babeque, I made directly south-east for Bohío.

Thursday, 6 December

At the hour of vespers we reached Bohío. It being that day the feast of San Nicolás, I named the port we entered Puerto San Nicolás. The harbour was better than all the ports of Juana, it being large, deep and full of canoes.

Sunday, 9 December

Seeing that the land and trees of this large island of Bohío resemble those of Spain, and the fish in the sailors' nets - salmon, hake and sardines - are also like those of Spain, I have named the island Española.

Wednesday 12 December

I set up a great cross on the west side of the entrance to the port as a sign of our Lord Jesus Christ. Three men who had gone off into the woods suddenly came across a great crowd of naked natives who immediately ran away. They managed to catch a very young and beautiful woman who wore a nose plug, and brought her to the ships. I gave her some trinkets and hawks' bells, before sending her back ashore unharmed and under the escort of three Spaniards and three Indians.

Thursday, 13 December

My three men had been too fearful of accompanying the girl right back to the village. Accordingly, to find out more about this land, I sent nine armed men ashore this morning. Four leagues into the interior, they found a village of more than a thousand huts, scattered about in a valley. The inhabitants fled to the woods when they saw the men, but the Indian from San Salvador persuaded them to return, whereupon they re-appeared. They were lighter skinned and more handsome than those on the other islands. Two girls had skins as white as any of those in Spain. They placed their hands on the crew's heads in a gesture of friendship, and brought bread and fish for them to eat. Others brought along parrots, for which they wanted nothing in exchange, and invited them to stay with them that night.

With regard to the beauty of this country, neither the best land in Castile, nor any of the lands we have seen so far, could be matched by it. There are very many sierras and lofty mountains, beyond comparison with the island of Tenerife. Trees there are of a thousand kinds, and so tall that they are a wonder to behold. It was the most pleasant place in the world. Española is a marvel.

Sunday, 16 December

Between Española and the island of Tortuga we met an Indian braving the rough sea in a small canoe. We took both him and his canoe on board and carried him to Española, giving him the usual gifts. He spoke so highly of us to the other Indians ashore that about five hundred of them, with their extremely youthful king, came out to the ship. These were the most beautiful men and women I have seen: stout, lusty and very pleasant. All they possessed of value were pieces of gold hanging from their ears and noses, but I learnt that there was more gold to the south.

In the afternoon, the king - a very young man - came on board, and I received him with due ceremony. I tried to explain that the ships belonged to the King and Queen of Castile, who were the greatest princes in the whole world. Like the Indians on board, however, he refused to believe any of this, insisting that we must have come from heaven, and that the monarchs must also rule ln heaven.

Monday, 17 December

The inhabitants drew my attention this morning to two men who had chunks of their flesh missing. They said that the cannibals were responsible but I didn't believe them.

In the afternoon, a large canoe wth forty Indians came over from Tortuga, an island which is supposed to contain more gold than Española. The natives immediately sat down, to show that they wanted peace; but most of the Indians in the canoe leaped ashore, as if they wanted to fight. The king of Española shouted threats at them, and then splashed water on them and threw stones at the canoe, until they turned back.

Tuesday, 18 December

Today was the Feast of the Annuniciation, and I ordered that the ship be adorned with arms and dressed in flags. The king was brought to the ship in a litter, carried by four men and accompanied by over two hundred attendants, all naked. When he came on board with all his people, I was dining at the table below the poop. He quickly came over to sit beside me, and insisted that I should continue with my meal. The other men sat outside on the deck, apart from two more senior advisers who sat at his feet. Thinking that he might like to eat some of our food, I ordered that some be brought to him Yet, of the dishes that were placed before him, he took of each only a taste. The rest he sent outside to his men. He did the same with his drink, raising it to his lips and then giving it to the others. All this he did in such a dignified way and in almost total silence.

After dinner, his attendant gave me a belt and two pieces of worked gold. I couldn't help noticing that these were very thin, and deduced that they are very poor in gold here. Nevertheless, I have been told that close by, there is plenty of gold, and even an island that is all gold. In return for his gifts, I gave the king the coverlet from my bed, some amber beads from around my neck, a pair of coloured shoes and a bottle of orange-flower water. He was obviously very pleased with these. When he left, I ordered that a gun be fired. I observed that his son was carried on the shoulders of a very important man, and that he, too, had a large retinue. Even the king's brother, who went on foot, had a great train of followers. I was especially delighted to see that all of the gifts I had given him were carried in front by a top official.

Sunday, 23 December

I continue to be very impressed by the people of these parts. Your Highnesses may believe that there is no better nor gentler people in the world. They love their neighbours as themselves, and they always speak with a smile. In the Cibao, which I believe to be Cipangu, they say that the king even carries banners of beaten gold.

Tuesday, 25 December

At eleven o'clock yesterday night, I retired to my cabin, having gone two days and a night without sleep. Some time around midnight, it being calm, and the helmsman believing that we were safe from reefs and shoals, a boy was allowed to take over the tiller. This I had expressly forbidden under any circumstances. As the crew slept, the ship was driven very gently onto a sand-bank which had gone quite unnoticed because of the dark. Suddenly, the boy cried out. I rushed up on deck and realised straight away that we had run aground. All this time, I could hear a terrific crashing of waves breaking on the reef. I ordered the men to board the boat which the ship was towing, and to cast anchor. Instead of this, they disobeyed me and rowed directly to the *Niña,* which refused to let them board. So as to lighten the ship, I had the mast cut down; but despite this and my best efforts to get her off the reef, she would not move. Instead, she listed, the seams opened, and she began to fill up with water. The people of Palos must carry a lot of the blame for providing such a heavy and unsuitable ship in the first place.

Now that it is evident that the *Santa María* cannot be saved, the crew have left to join the *Niña.* A boat was also sent ashore to let the king know what had happened. On hearing our bad news, he was reduced to tears and sent all his people in large canoes to the ship, so as to help unload. Sharing in our misfortune, they also wept. Once unloaded, the king most generously let us use two houses for storage, and has posted armed men to keep watch, day and night, over our goods.

Wednesday, 26 December

The king came to the *Niña* and offered me all he had. While he was talking to us, some Indians arrived in a canoe from another place. They came with pieces of gold leaf which they bartered for needles and hawks' bells which they highly prized. The king dined with me on shrimps and cassava bread, before going ashore. He gave me some masks with golden eyes and with large ears of gold. In exchange for these, I gave him a pair of gloves and a shirt. He also promised me four pieces of gold the size of a man's hand, and a lot more gold from the Cibao region.

All of these kindnesses and gifts helped to ease the loss of my flagship. In truth, from this mishap originated so many things that it was really a piece of good fortune. If God had not brought about the sinking, we should never have been able to make a settlement here. On my next voyage it will prove an excellent base.

After the meal, the king accompanied me to the beach. Here, I showed him a bow and arrows. After giving due warning, I took a shot at one of my men. The king had no weapons like these, and was absolutely amazed. I also ordered that the ship's cannon be fired, and the Indians were so terrified at the noise that they fell down as if dead. I told the king that his people must use these weapons to defend themselves against the Caribs who were forever capturing them and carrying them away to eat.

I have given instructions that a tower and a fort be built out of timber from the ship. Many men have offered to make their homes here and man such a fort [see *Plate 15*]; although I believe that with the force I have with me I could subjugate the whole island. On my return here, I expect them to have collected a tun of gold by barter. They should also have found the gold mine by that time, and so much spice that within three years your Highnesses will be able to equip an expedition to go and conquer the Holy Sepulchre.

Thursday, 27 December

A report that the *Pinta* was in a river at the eastern end of the island was shown to be unfounded.

Saturday, 29 December

A very young nephew of the king told me that to the east, on an island called either Guarionex, or Mayoric, or Mayonic, or Fuma, or Cibao, or Coroay, there was plenty of gold. I carefully noted down all these names. It may be that the king had known about these places all along but did not want me to go and barter elsewhere.

Tonight I exchanged a washhand basin and jug for a large mask of gold.

Sunday, 30 December

I went on shore to dinner. There were no less than five kings besides the one I knew, who was called Guacanagarí. All wore crowns. After this, Guacanagarí took me to a house where, seated on a couch, he took off his crown and placed it on my head. In return, I took some coloured beads from around my neck and put them on the king. I also placed my coat around him, and sent off for some coloured boots; while on his finger I put a large silver ring which he much admired.

When I returned to the *Niña*, Vicente Yáñez Pinzón told me that he had seen the rhubarb plant on the island of Amiga.

15. Building a fort at La Navidad, Española

Monday, 31 December

Water and fuel were taken on board ready for the return voyage to Spain. Before
departing, I had hoped to examine the east of the island, to see whether we might

send out sheep and cattle from Spain. Unfortunately, because we had been left with only one vessel due to Pinzón's treachery, I felt that this move was probably unwise.

Tuesday, 1 January 1493

At midnight, I sent a boat to the island of Amiga to bring back the rhubarb. It returned at the time of evening prayer with a bundle of it. The men did not bring more because they had no spade to dig it up with. I am taking it back to Spain with me to show your Highnesses.

Twenty leagues away, there is supposed to be a king who wears large plates of gold on his head.

There is still no news of the *Pinta*.

Wednesday, 2 January

I entrusted a total of forty-four men to run and garrison the fort. They included a ship's carpenter, a caulker, a cooper, a physician, a tailor and a gunner. So that, in time, the men could go off to discover the gold mine, I decided to leave the ship's boat behind.

To show King Guacanagarí once again the strength of our weapons, I ordered that a lombard shot be fired through the side of the *Niña;* it went far out to sea.

Thursday, 3 January

My departure was delayed by the late return of three Indians whom I had sent ashore. I am praying for favourable weather, for I am determined to depart tomorrow, God willing. There will be no further stops to discover more islands, in case some accident should prevent me returning to Castile altogether, and spreading my news. My fury with Martín Alonso Pinzón for letting me down knows no bounds. I would not be surprised if he tried to arrive back before me and tell lies to your Majesties, so as to avoid being punished for his treachery.

Friday, 4 January

I set off at sunrise, steering north-west in a rough sea, amidst extensive reefs and shoals. The town I left behind me I named Villa de la Navidad, for I had reached it on Christmas Day. It has the distinction of being the first Christian town in the Indies.

I steered in the direction of Monte Cristi, a very high mountain which seemed to come up out of the sea like an island. About six leagues from Monte Cristi, I anchored. I am sure that Cipangu is somewhere in that island.

Sunday, 6 January

The *Pinta* was sighted. Its wilful captain, Martín Alonso Pinzón, came up to and boarded the *Niña*. He didn't say one word about the gold that had lured him away. Instead, he invented a host of excuses for having separated from me. I didn't believe a single word he said, knowing the man to be hostile, disloyal and downright disobedient. Nevertheless, I thought it best to pretend to believe him because the crew were mostly from Pinzón's own town, and some were his own relatives. I heard that near the Río de Gracia, west of Navidad, he had found a lot of gold, some pieces the size of two fingers, and had divided half of it amongst his crew and kept half for himself. Of course, he tried to convince me that he knew nothing of this. He had also taken by force four men and two girls who I now ordered should be put on shore so that they could return to their homes.

Monday, 7 January

The men cut wood and caulked the *Niña*. Much aloe and mastic was collected.

Tuesday, 8 January

Delayed from setting sail by an east wind, I took the boat up a river to the south-west of Monte Cristi. Here, the men got fresh water for the ships. On finding much gold dust, and later on grains of gold as large as lentils, I decided to name the river Río del Oro. No less wonderfully, I saw three mermaids rising out of the sea. Each had a kind of human face but they are not as beautiful as the painted ones I've seen.

My main aim is now to bring news back to Spain, and to rid myself of this evil company, who are a mutinous bunch at best.

Wednesday, 9 January

Tonight, I shall set out on my homeward voyage without any further delay. I can no longer suffer the deeds and disrespect of ill-disposed persons who seem to forget that they owe their position to me in the first place. Still, I have found what I was after, and I don't wish to argue any more with Martín Alonso until your Highnesses should know all the news of the voyage.

Sunday, 13 January

For the last few days, I have skirted the coast of Española and have been astonished at the great size of this island. Today, in Samaná Bay, I encountered some very ferocious and ugly Indians. They were armed with bows and arrows, and spoke as if very angry. Their faces were stained with charcoal and they wore their hair long and gathered behind their head into nets made from parrot's feathers. One of them eventually came aboard, and indicated rather haughtily that pieces of gold the size of the poop of the *Niña* could be found over to the east. This was the direction in which the Caribs lived.

At certain times of the year, the Caribs sleep with women on the island of Martininó. If the women bear daughters they are allowed to keep them, but if they produce sons they are given to their fathers on their fourteenth birthday. Hoping to win their friendship, and believing that they might lead us to gold, I gave the man some glass beads and some pieces of green and red cloth.

At first, all seemed well, for when we went ashore he managed to persuade the other Indians to lay down their bows and arrows and their large cudgels. However, suddenly they fetched cord and were intent on tying up the hands of my crew. We were ready for this attack, and though only seven in number compared with fifty-five of them, my men charged at the Indians, slashing one on the buttocks with a sword, and wounding another in the breast with an arrow. These people being Caribs, I feel we were justified in our behaviour. Leaving behind most of their bows and arrows, the Indians then turned and fled. This was a pity because I should like to have captured some of them. I am beginning to fear for the safety of my men at La Navidad.

Wednesday, 16 January

The weather being fair, I set sail from this bay - which I have named Golfo de las Flechas [Bay of Arrows] - bound for Castile. This was all to the great satisfaction of my men. I hope to go by way of the island of Martininó and take from there five or six of those women who live without men.

Wednesday, 23 January

The *Niña* often has to wait for the *Pinta,* as her mizzen is now almost useless because of her weak mast. Indeed, if her captain, Martín Alonso Pinzón, had taken the precaution of providing her with a good mast in the Indies, instead of deserting his commander through sheer greed, there would not have been a problem now.

Wednesday, 13 February

The wind has raged all day, and the sea has been high and tempestuous. Lightning struck three times. At one point the wind moderated, but later it increased again.

Thursday, 14 February

All night the ships have been completely at the mercy of the wind. The *Pinta,* for the reasons I have given, being especially vulnerable, has scudded north. I made flames all night but by daybreak I had lost sight of her. It seems she must have capsized. After saying prayers, we drew lots, using chick-peas, to decide who should make a pilgrimage to the shrine of Our Lady of Guadalupe, carrying with him a six pound candle. Then lots were drawn to make a pilgrimage to Our Lady of Loreto, and to perform night watch at the Church of Santa Clara de Moguer near Palos. In two of these cases, the chick-pea with the cross on it was drawn by myself.

As the storm worsened, the whole crew vowed to go barefoot and in their shirts to the first shrine of the Virgin they should encounter, and there say their prayers. None of us are now expecting to escape with our lives.

As the provisions have almost been consumed, the ship has no proper ballast. To help compensate for this, my men filled up all the empty water casks with sea water, so as to make the ship more stable. Please God that our hopes at this late stage be not dashed. I continually think of my two sons at school in Córdoba. Is it possible that God could be punishing me for my little faith, snatching glory away from me in my final hour? My spirits are certainly not lifted by the men grumbling and wishing that they had not come with me after all.

Thinking that I might never return to Castile, and that my news might never be known, I have written a brief report on a piece of parchment about how I discovered the lands and have given the route and length of the voyage, together with some details about the lands and their inhabitants. A reward of one thousand ducats is offered to whoever should deliver it, sealed, to your Highnesses. I wrapped the parchment in a cake of wax and dropped it into a wooden barrel. I then threw it into the sea. To be doubly certain that it reaches your Highnesses, I have placed a similar barrel at the ship's stern.

Friday, 15 February

By morning, the sky had begun to clear but the sea was still very high. Some of the men claimed to see Madeira, others the Rock of Cintra in Portugal. A few of the more hopeful ones even thought it was Castile. I told them it was one of the Azores. Although the island is not far away, we were prevented by the storm from reaching it today.

Saturday, 16 February

With the storm still raging, we reached the island which was hidden in a great mist.

Sunday, 17 February

Last night, I managed to rest a little, not having slept since Wednesday. My legs are weak from being exposed to the wet and cold.

Monday, 18 February

The natives thanked God for our miraculous escape from the tempest which they said had raged for a fortnight. Three of them came to the ship with food and drink, and were overjoyed when they learnt that I had discovered the Indies. This island is called Santa María.

Tuesday, 19 February

Today, the whole crew fulfilled their promise to go barefoot and in their shirts to the first shrine dedicated to the Virgin. The priest got the keys and I ordered that first half the crew, and then the other half, should hear mass. No sooner had the first half landed, ready to go to the shrine, than they were ambushed and made prisoners. The boat which had taken them ashore was also seized. I knew nothing of this until about eleven o'clock when I was becoming anxious, seeing as the men had left at dawn. I sailed around to where I could see the shrine, and to my horror saw horsemen dismount and get into the boat with arms. I immediately told my own men to arm themselves and be on guard. When the boat's captain returned, I questioned him on the whereabouts of the rest of my men. He replied that by taking them captive he was only obeying the orders of the King of Portugal. At this I was enraged. I referred to my great commission from your Highnesses, and my important rank of Admiral of the Ocean Sea and Viceroy of the Indies. I told him quite plainly that if he did not release my men, I should in any case continue back to Seville, and then he would be severely dealt with. The captain and his men replied that they knew nothing about any such commission, and that they were not afraid of the King and Queen of Castile. On hearing this, I swore that I would not leave until a hundred Portuguese had been captured and the island laid waste.

Wednesday, 20 February

In another great wind - a frequent thing in these parts - I lost anchor and had to sail for San Miguel.

Thursday, 21 February

I lay dangerously at sea last night, desperate for shelter. The crew now being so few in number, I have to do most of the work myself.

The weather being calmer this morning, I endeavoured to sail back to Santa María in order to recover my men, anchors and boat. In the afternoon, soon after I had reached the island, a boat came alongside carrying five seamen, two priests and a notary. They boarded the ship after I had given them assurances of safety. As it was late, they are sleeping on board.

Friday, 22 February

The men who came aboard yesterday said that they had been sent to learn more about what our business was. I showed them the letter from your Highnesses and the commission I had been given to undertake the voyage. Now satisfied, the Portuguese saw to the return of my men and my boat. They explained that if they had also captured me, as the King of Portugal had intended, then my men would not have been released.

Sunday, 24 February

Unsuccessful in finding wood and stones to act as ballast for the ships, we left Santa María on an easterly course for Castile. The wind was favourable.

Sunday, 3 March

Such a ferocious tempest has blown today that it has split our sails. We drew lots once more to see who should go as a pilgrim, barefoot and in his shirt, to the shrine of Santa María de la Cinta in Huelva. The lot fell on me again. The whole crew promised to fast on bread and water on the first Saturday after our return. This evening we forced ourselves on, amidst thunder and lightning. Some time around midnight, I sighted land.

Monday, 4 March

At daybreak, I saw that we were near the Rock of Cintra in Portugal. The people there had been praying for our safety, and were overjoyed that our ship had escaped such a bad storm. I entered the estuary of Lisbon and anchored off Restello, from where I wrote a letter to the King of Portugal, asking for permission to anchor at Lisbon. At the same time I sent a messenger to your Highnesses to announce our return.

Tuesday, 5 March

The master of the port of Restello, Bartolomé Diaz, came alongside us in an armed boat, and insisted that I come with him to give an account of myself before the King's ministers. I replied that no admirals of the King of Castile had to obey any such summons. Indeed, they are not allowed to leave their ships, nor even to send a deputy. Relenting, the master demanded to see my credentials which he took with him to show his own captain, Alvaro Dama. He was so impressed to see the letter from your Highnesses that he came on board with trumpets, fifes and drums to congratulate me and to offer his services.

Wednesday, 6 March

A huge number of people swarmed aboard at Lisbon to see the Indians, and to hear the story of the discovery. Indeed, the water could not be seen because of all the boats. But some of the Portuguese were angry that their own King had turned down the opportunity of commissioning such an enterprise.

Friday, 8 March

The King of Portugal has invited me to visit him. Despite some misgivings, I agreed, and went to Valparaiso where he was staying. My crew and myself were supplied with provisions at the King's own expense.

Saturday, 9 March

Tonight, as the rain beat down, I reached Valparaiso where I was greeted by all the nobles of the court and treated with great courtesy and friendliness, being asked to sit and told it was unnecessary to doff my cap. The King was delighted that the voyage had been successful; but claimed that because of a treaty which he had with Spain, all of the lands I had discovered belonged to him! I replied that I knew nothing of such a treaty and had been very careful to avoid going near any Portuguese possessions.

Tuesday, 12 March

After dinner yesterday I left the Prior of Clato with whom I had lodged. Accompanied by Don Martín de Noroña and a great escort, still eager to hear my stories, I departed for Lisbon. On my way I stopped to see the Queen of Portugal who was staying in a monastery at Villafranca, and was delighted to see me.

Wednesday, 13 March

I have been offered lodgings and a supply of mules to go to Seville by land but I decided to go by sea, setting sail at eight o'clock this morning.

Friday, 15 March

At noon, I anchored in the harbour of Palos, seven months and twelve days after my departure on 3 August 1492. The inhabitants were so proud because most of the crew came from their town. Hearty thanks were offered to God who has shown his favour in the successful outcome of this voyage which promises to greatly advance the Christian religion.

Pinzón had already arrived in Galicia, and proposed to go on his own to Barcelona to give an account of the voyage to the King and Queen of Spain; but they refused to see him without Columbus. In the event, he died shortly after his return to Palos.

In mid-April Columbus reached Barcelona. Along the road he was met by admiring crowds, eager to see not just him but also the Indians and souvenirs of the voyage. At court he was seated on a grand throne under a canopy of cloth of gold, and treated like a great lord. There he gave a brief account of the voyage, after which the whole court accompanied him to his lodgings. The next day, as a mark of distinction, Columbus rode on one side of the King as he rode about Barcelona.

Summary chart of important events in the First Voyage

3 August 1492	The *Santa María,* the *Niña,* and the *Pinta* set sail from Palos, Spain
12 August	The ships reached the Canaries
16 September	The crew saw a great mass of weed. Further signs of land also turned out to be false alarms
11 October	At 10 p.m. Columbus thought he saw a light in the distance
12 October	The three captains went ashore and lay claim to San Salvador
15 October - 21 October	The islands of Santa María, Fernandina and Isabella were all taken before setting sail in search of Cuba
21 November	Martín Alonso Pinzón parted company with the others
6 December	Columbus landed at Española
25 December	The *Santa María* was wrecked on a reef
6 January 1493	Pinzón rejoined Columbus
14 February	A terrible storm separated the *Niña* and the *Pinta*
19 February	Half the crew of the *Niña* were ambushed by the Portuguese in the Azores
15 March	Columbus returned to Palos without Pinzón

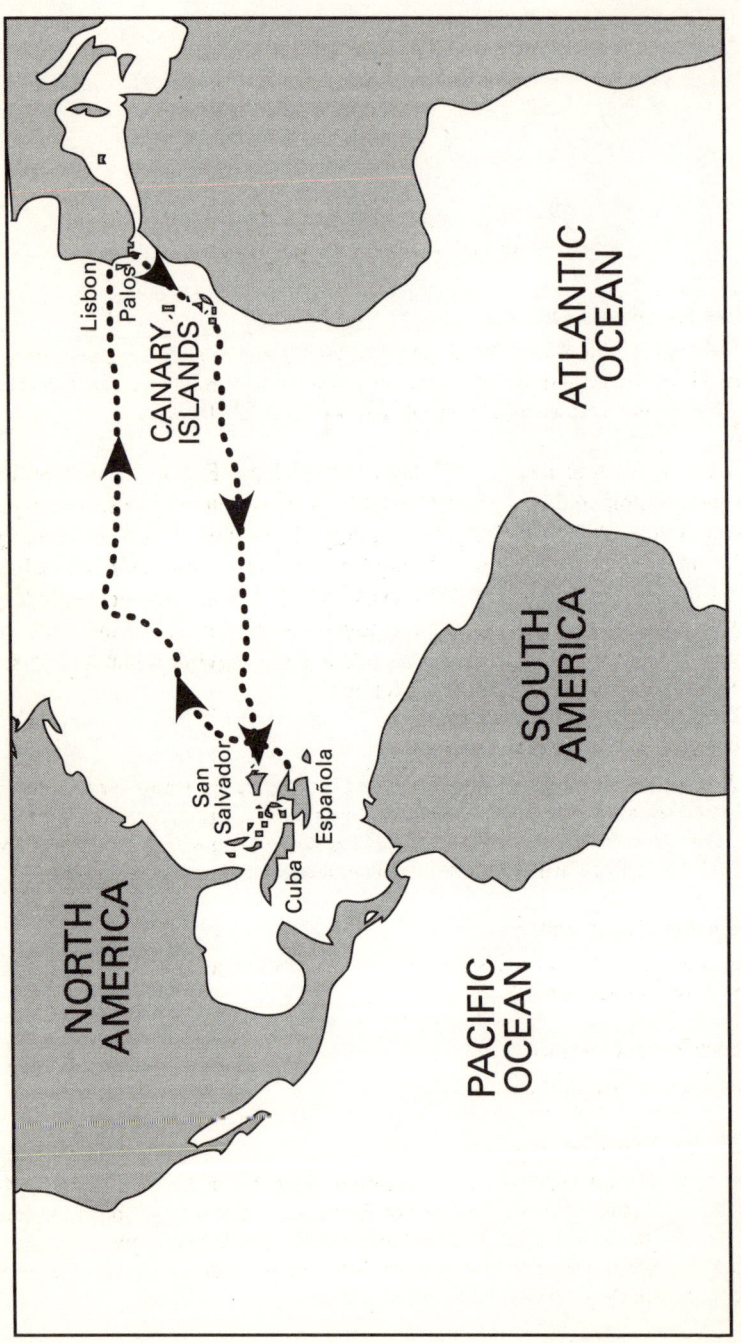

16. The route of Columbus's First Voyage, 1492-3

Chapter VI

The Second Voyage, 1493-6:
Rejoice and Conquer

Tuesday, 28 May 1493

I have received instructions from the King and Queen to return to Española and complete the conquest. All of my former privileges have been renewed. I shall be taking out more settlers and relieving those who are already there.

The following month, Columbus sailed from Barcelona to Seville, where he prepared a much-improved fleet of seventeen ships, the larger ones roomy enough to carry horses, cows and sheep; others sufficiently shallow to explore inlets. A huge number of volunteers wished to accompany him, from which he chose some fifteen hundred, including his brother, Don Diego, who he appointed second in command; and the eminent doctor and physician, Diego Chanca of Seville. Members of the Pinzón family were deliberately excluded.

Wednesday, 25 September

All preparations complete and prayers said, I weighed anchor in fair weather in Cádiz harbour. With bright banners flying from the rigging and the sound of trumpets and cannon fire echoing around the shore, I began to steer a course for the Canary Islands, where I shall take on more supplies.

Saturday, 28 September

An abundance of small land birds and turtle-doves came to the ship *en route* from the Azores to Africa for the winter.

Wednesday, 2 October

Repairs were made off Grand Canary.

Monday, 7 October

We took on fresh supplies - meat, firewood, water and fodder; some more animals; and a range of fruit to cultivate on Española. At last we left Gomera and set course for the Indies - first west, and then west by south. I have given each captain sealed instructions on how to reach Navidad, but ordered that these only be opened if we should be separated in bad weather.

Saturday, 26 October

St Simon's Eve. Tonight there was heavy rain and terrifying thunder. The crew sang litanies and said prayers to St Elmo for protection. Soon after this the sea became as smooth as polished marble. My men yearn for the sight of land.

Saturday, 2 November

Earlier today, the presence of birds flying westwards and of dark, threatening clouds ahead convinces me that land is near. I have given orders for all ships to shorten sail.

Sunday, 3 November

Sure enough, at dawn an island was sighted to the west of us, the first of many islands. My men, though exhausted with pumping out water, were delighted beyond all measure at the sight of land, and clambered on deck, where we prayed and sang the *Salve Regina*. Seeing as we have discovered it on a Sunday morning, I am naming this high, mountainous island Dominica. The next island, which is flat and covered with very thick, lush trees, I have named María Galante after my flagship.

Monday, 4 November

I left María Galante and sailed northward toward another huge island which I named Santa María de Guadalupe, thereby fulfilling my promise to name an island after a monastery. In the distance we saw a mighty waterfall.

First, we visited a town which was visible from the beach. Apart from some children, its inhabitants had fled. We gave the children hawks' bells, to convince their parents of our good intent. The houses were full of geese and large parrots of a variety of colours. The natives had those canvas beds which were supported at each end by a post, and owned bows and arrows which they used to defend themselves. Being good Christians, I assure you that we left all these things untouched.

Tuesday, 5 November

I sent two boats ashore, with orders to find out more about this country, and how to get from here to Española and on to Cathay. Each boat returned with a young Indian, not natives of this island but from another land, having been captured by the men from Guadalupe, who are Caribs. Later, six women who had fled from the Caribs came to the ships. We presented them with glass beads and hawks' bells but these were seized by the Caribs.

When we returned for food and water, the women begged us to take them aboard, so freeing them from the Caribs who were then on a raiding expedition, and who kept them as slaves. My men took them aboard, along with two children and a young man who had escaped from the Caribs, who are always raiding islands and stealing people to eat.

One woman told us that to the south there are many islands, some of which are inhabited : one of the islands is two thirds gold. We were given directions to Española, and I charted its position.

Thursday, 7 November

For two days now I have heard nothing of a party of eight men, led by Captain Márquez, which had gone ashore without my permission. Search parties, equipped with trumpets and harquebuses, have failed to find any trace of them in the dense forest. I dread to think what may have happened to them in the hands of the Caribs. I have a good mind to continue with the voyage without them, as a warning to others, but the mens' friends and relatives begged me to stay on. I ordered that the time be used to good advantage in washing clothes and loading on board more wood and water. I sent Captain Alonso de Hojeda ashore with forty men to search for them, but they have just returned, bringing back only aloe, ginger, incense, cotton and a variety of birds.

Friday, 8 November

The party which had left ship without my permission has turned up and claimed that they had lost their way in the thick forest. I ordered that they all be punished : the captain has been put in chains, and the others have been put on short rations.

I went ashore before leaving. In some houses I saw skulls hanging from the ceiling, and baskets full of men's bones.

Sunday, 10 November

I took the fleet north-west along the coast of Guadalupe towards Española. We passed by an island with lofty peaks, to which I gave the name Montserrat. The Indians on board told me that the Caribs had eaten all of the island's inhabitants. Later, we passed an island so round and smooth that I named it Santa María la Redonda.

Thursday, 14 November

Although anxious to relieve the men we had left on Española, fierce winds forced me to lay anchor. I sent out a boat to seek help. As the boat was returning, it encountered a canoe carrying four men (all of whom had been castrated by the Caribs) and a woman who fired arrows with such strength that they passed through a shield. The boat rammed the canoe so that the canoe overturned. Even now, whilst swimming, one of the Indians still fired arrows, mortally wounding one of our men. But they were no match for my men who brought them aboard as captives. One of them is certain to die from a stomach wound.

We continued to sail north-west, and on the island of San Juan Bautista [Puerto Rico] we found well-built Indian houses, grouped around a plaza, with a wide road bordered by cane turrets, leading to a watchtower by the sea.

17. Cannibals [from Thevet *Singularitez* (1558)]

[The cannibals (Caribs) castrated boys and fattened them up for the cooking pot. Roast baby was an even greater delicacy for them.]

Friday, 22 November

I reached the northern shore of Española, and sent one of the Indians ashore at Samaná Bay. A convert to Christianity himself, I am happy that he agreed to convert the others.

A party which went ashore at the harbour of Monte Cristi discovered a terrifying omen : two dead men (one with traces of a typically Spanish beard) on the banks of a river, the older with a rope around his neck and his hands tied to a wooden cross.

Today, we buried the seaman who had been fatally wounded in the fight with the Caribs.

Tuesday, 26 November

The Indians came out to speak to us showing no signs of fear, touching our clothes and naming each article. Their friendly behaviour convinced me that they had not harmed the Christians we had found drowned.

Wednesday, 27 November

Two Indians came to the ship's side in a canoe and came aboard. Each had a mask over his face which they presented to me with greetings from their cacique,

Guacanagarí. In return, I gave them metal basins for the cacique and his family. They told me that some of the Christians at Navidad had died of sickness and that others had moved on. I was horrified to hear that all have four or five wives each.

Thursday, 28 November

I learnt to my great dismay and horror that the town of Navidad had been burned to the ground and was utterly destitute of people. I can scarcely believe what has happened.

Friday, 29 November

It greatly saddens me to see the ruins of the houses and the fort - a sorry picture of devastation indeed. Furthermore, all the gold I had ordered put in the well of the fort for safekeeping had disappeared. In all, I found the bodies of eleven Christians who seemed to have been dead for about a month.

The Indians had fled into the woods but later the cacique's brother and some other Indians explained that soon after I had left Navidad on my first voyage there were quarrels to get as much gold and as many women as possible.

Another cacique, called Caonabó, had brought an army to Navidad one night and set fire to the Christians' houses. Some of the Christians had rushed to the sea and were drowned. Guacanagarí himself claimed he had been wounded, though I am suspicious about these injuries, and about his possible involvement in the plot.

Saturday, 30 November

The cacique told how he and his men had been attacked with spears and arrows. He presented me with some small coloured stone beads, some gold beads and a gold crown. When he accompanied me to the fleet, he was absolutely fascinated by the sight of the horses. I told him about Christian law, and gave him a silver image of the Virgin which he now wears around his neck.

Sunday, 8 December

After cruising amongst the many islands in these parts, I anchored in a very fine harbour - directly in front of an Indian village - and went ashore.

From 11 December 1493 until 12 March 1494 Columbus was ill and did not keep a journal. On 2 January 1494 the fleet dropped anchor off what appeared to be a sheltered peninsula which offered plenty of opportunities for fishing. On 6 January Mass was celebrated ashore.

The settlement which Columbus founded here was laid out on Spanish lines, and was called Isabela in honour of the Queen. Columbus lost no time in sending out Alonso de Hojeda with fifteen men to the Cibao in search of the gold mines. Wherever they went the caciques were hospitable and they returned with a lot of gold which they found in brooks. Columbus believed that he must now be getting close to Cathay, and decided to go in search of gold himself.

In early February, twelve ships under the charge of Antonio de Torres, and carrying a cargo of spices, wood and Indians, left for Castile, to report back to the King and Queen.

Wednesday, 12 March 1494

While I was ill, that knave Bernal de Pisa, being too lazy to work on building the new town and also very greedy for gold, had mutinied. To prevent another episode of this kind, I ordered that all weapons be stored in the flagship.

I left Isabela for the mines of the Cibao with a great body of men, sporting trumpets and banners, and firing guns - a force more than a match for the Indians. On the march we skirted wooded mountains, saw the first decent road built in the Indies and passed through many Indian villages full of round thatched huts.

Some of the Indians we brought with us went into the huts and helped themselves to anything which took their fancy. Of course, when the natives tried to do the same to my men, they were rebuffed.

Friday, 14 March

We crossed a large river which I named the Río de Oro, on account of the gold dust it contained. Soon after this, we came to a village. Some of the people had fled to the hills but the majority had shut themselves up and had bolted the doors of their huts.

Sunday, 16 March

I entered the Cibao - a rough and stony region as large as Portugal and found gold dust in the mountain streams At Santo Tomás I ordered that a fort be built such as could command a dominating position, and placed Pedro Margarit with fifty-six men in control. In a river beneath the hill where the fort is to stand, we found marble and jasper.

Friday, 21 March

I set off for Isabela. Torrential rain making it quite impossible to cross the Río Verde and the Río de Oro, I toured the Indian villages instead, living off a diet of cassava bread and yams.

Saturday, 29 March

I arrived back at Isabela. To my amazement, the melons we planted less than two months ago are now ready to eat, and the cucumbers have come up in three weeks. But there is much else to make me unhappy - a number of men have died, and the provisions we brought from Spain have almost run out.

Sunday, 30 March

I am very impressed with the climate and the fertility of this country, its soft, healthy water, and its abundance of wheat, fruit and sugar cane.

Tuesday 1 April

A messenger arrived to say that Caonabó was on the point of burning the fort at Santo Tomás. I shall be sending Pedro Margarit reinforcements and provisions. Nevertheless, I do not put much stock in this report, knowing how feeble the Indians are. They will run a mile when they see one of our horses, for they believe that they can fly across rivers.

Wednesday, 2 April

I sent twenty-five men, with food and ammunition, to garrison the fort, and a further forty-five to build a new road. The thin air and the Indian food do not agree with my men, but they must get used to it.

Whilst the caravels are being repaired, I am supervising work on the town of Isabela, dividing it into streets which meet in a spacious square, and digging a wide channel down to the river.

I have ordered that some gristmills be built, for we are out of flour. The trouble is that the workmen are a naturally idle bunch and are forever shirking work. I have to watch over them the whole time.

I shall be leaving three hundred men on the island, and shall send the rest back to Castile. Hojeda will relieve Margarit as governor at Santo Tomás.

Wednesday, 9 April

Today, Hojeda left for Santo Tomás with more than a hundred men. At the Río de Oro he captured a cacique and his brother, and sent them both back to me in chains. He also cut off the ears of one of the cacique's subjects, as his people had stolen our clothes. I was ready to sentence the culprits to death when another cacique intervened on their behalf, and shed so many tears that I set them free, on the promise that they would not offend again.

Thursday, 24 April

Shortly after noon, I boarded the *Niña* and, in company wlth the *San Juan* and *Cordera,* left this golden isle in the hands of my brother, Diego and a council of four others. Having explored the coastline, I anchored that evening at Monte Cristi.

Sunday, 27 April

I cast forth from Navidad, having waited two days in vain to see the cacique Guacanagarí.

Tuesday, 29 April

It being fair weather, I reached Puerto San Nicolás and then crossed to Juana [Cuba]. I cannot be sure whether this is an island or part of the mainland of Cathay. I anchored in a large bay which I have named Puerto Grande, and dined on fish and hutias.

Thursday, 1 May

I carried on cruising down the coast, finding large harbours, beautiful rivers and lofty mountains all the way. The Indians, who greeted us in their canoes, thought we had come from heaven, and brought us cassava bread, water and fish. I insisted that these be exchanged for glass beads and hawks' bells.

Saturday, 3 May

I cast off from Cabo de Cruz at the south western tip of Juana, and steered a course for Jamaica which I believe to be very rich in gold.

Tuesday 6 May

Having anchored off Jamaica yesterday, I cruised along its coast today and took note of its beautiful harbours. As our boats passed one harbour, a huge number of very large canoes came out. Anxious to avoid hostilities with the Indians, I ordered the boats to return. At another harbour, the Indians came out and hurled darts at us. This time, they got what they deserved. I released a hound, and my crossbowmen wounded half a dozen Indians, forcing them to retreat. After this, there was a period of peace, during which time much trading went on.

Tuesday, 13 May

The island of Jamaica is surely the loveliest and most graceful of all that I have seen so far, and, above all, the most rich in gold. Shortly, I intend to return to Juana, to determine whether it is an island or part of the mainland. As I was preparing to sail, a young Indian begged us to take him to Castile, and hid on board, much to the unhappiness of his family. Impressed by his courage, I agreed to give him passage, and ordered my crew to treat him well.

Wednesday, 14 May

We returned to Cape Santa Cruz in the throes of a terrible storm. I really had my work cut out, what with this and the abundance of tiny islands barely visible above the water.

Thursday, 15 May

I counted a maze of some one hundred and sixty islets today, but most of them larger than those we saw yesterday. I have called them collectively the Queen's Garden - each one is surely full of marvels. The number of turtles and bright red cranes in these parts is a wonder to behold. As for the air, it is beautifully sweet here. So near must we now be to Cathay.

We saw some Indians fishing in a most unusual manner. They tie threads to certain fish which they use as bait. These sucking fish stick tight to the neck of other fish, so that when they pull in the line they retrieve both fish together. Later on, at a nearby village, we were presented with one of these fish, and also offered some roast barkless dog. More than this I refused to accept from the Indians.

Monday, 19 May

I confess that I have not undressed and had a proper night's sleep since leaving Spain.

Tuesday, 20 May

Today, we sighted more than seventy-one islands as we continued to sail west. These make navigation difficult, particularly as every afternoon they are shrouded in a thick mist. This mist is always accompanied by terrible thunder and lightning.

Thursday, 22 May

We landed at a fair-sized island, which I named Santa Marta. As usual, we found that all the Indians had run away. In their huts we found dogs, like mastiffs, and a lot of fish which both the Indians and the dogs feed upon. Finding no one to talk to anywhere, I navigated through another labyrinth of islands - all tiring work - and even though I took the greatest care, the ship scraped the bottom from time to time.

We must now return to the island of Juana for more water.

Friday, 23 May

One of my sailors, who went hunting in the woods, reported that he had come across thirty Indians carrying darts and clubs. All were dressed in white tunics and appeared to have just as light a complexion as our men. But he wasted a chance to speak to them by calling for help and causing them to run away.
I sent a party ashore to try and check the sailor's story, but they could not get far on account of the dense forests and the marshes. All they saw were a few fishermen on the beach and some large cranes.

Tuesday, 10 June

I detained an Indian until he promised to give me some information about Juana. He said that it was an island (though I did not believe him); and that sign language was used to convey instructions from the cacique to the people.

Wednesday, 11 June

There are so many small channels of water in these parts. I had to have the ship towed over a sandbank into a deeper channel.

Thursday, 12 June

We remain at anchor off Juana. Surely this is the start of the mainland of the Indies. The sea is covered with large turtles. We saw above us this morning such a huge number of cormorants that they darkened the sun.

Friday, 13 June

I have come to realise that Juana certainly extends very far - too far for an island - and the islands surrounding it seem to go on for ever. Food is running out and my men are very gloomy. It is God's judgement that we should return and avoid the terrible uncertainties of what might follow. After taking on food and water at the island of San Juan Evangelista, I have now decided to turn back to my new town of Isabela on Española.

So many butterflies have flown around the ship all day that they have filled the air, until a heavy rain earlier this evening blew them away.

Wednesday 25 June

We have at last left Evangelista, and are sailing north-west in the direction of some small islands off Juana. The sea has been at first frothy green and white; then, as white as milk, though cloudy underneath; and finally, as black as ink.

Monday, 30 June

We continue to be plagued by many channels... My ship was running aground even as I was making the last entry in my log. Not being able to get her off by the stern, we managed, with God's aid, to pull her off by the bow; but the ship has suffered considerable damage from the impact. To make matters worse, we have had to endure violent squalls of rain all the way to the coast of Juana, where the air was once more full of the scent of flowers.

Monday, 7 July

I went on shore and heard Mass. Here, the local cacique indicated by signs that the good would go to heaven, and the wicked would go to hell. He also told us that he had travelled to western Juana where the cacique dressed like a priest.

Wednesday, 16 July

Near Cape Cruz, off Juana, there was such an outburst of rain and thunder that the deck was flooded. With God's help, we were able to anchor, but so much water kept pouring down through the deck that my sailors could not pump it out quickly enough. This was partly because they were too weak, their only food - and mine - being rotten biscuits and wine. Even if they are lucky enough to catch a fish, they cannot keep it more than a day because it goes off so easily.

All this hardship is in the service of God and that of your Highnesses. Otherwise, we would not be willing to endure such pains and dangers; for not a day passes when we do not look death in the face.

Friday, 18 July

We were welcomed on our arrival at Cape Cruz by some Indians who brought us a great amount of cassava bread, fish and fruit.

Tuesday, 22 July

The wind being unfavourable to return to Española, I made for Jamaica once again.

On the way, we were greeted by a local cacique wearing a cloak of red feathers and carrying a white banner. His wife and two daughters came with him and asked whether they could be taken back to Spain. I could not agree with their request, there being little enough food for us as it is. To console the cacique, I said that we would take him next time.

Jamaica is a most beautiful, green and fertile land, with plenty of splendid harbours. I have cruised down the west of the island and was treated with the utmost hospitality by the natives who came out in their boats with food. There seems, however, to be no gold.

Each afternoon there have been squalls of rain which have forced me to take shelter near the land. I would like to stay longer but the leaky state of the ships and the shortage of provisions make this impossible. In any case, there is still no word of any gold.

Tuesday, 19 August

The weather having improved, I left Jamaica and sailed east towards Española.

Wednesday, 20 August

Having sailed about thirty miles, I reached what I presumed to be the western end of Española, and named it the Cape of San Miguel.

Saturday, 23 August

I was greeted in person by a cacique who spoke some Spanish to me. This proved beyond all doubt that this is indeed Española.

Towards the end of August, Columbus anchored at a small island which he named Alta Vela. Having completely lost sight of the other two ships, he sent some men ashore to climb to the top of a hill. Still there was no trace of them, and they did not turn up until almost a week later. Then the small fleet continued on down the coast.

At one village where they stopped for fresh water, the Indians came out armed with bows and poisoned arrows, and threatened to tie the Spaniards up. But when the Indians saw that they meant them no harm, they were friendly enough, brought the visitors bread and water, and talked to them. As they left, the sailors caught sight of an enormous fish, as large as a whale. Its head was the size of a barrel, it had a long tail (like that of a tunny) and two large wings.

Monday, 15 September

After some really foul weather, God showed his favour by leading us to a channel between Española and another island to its east (which the Indians call Adamaney) where we could take shelter. I fear for the safety of the other two ships, for they were unable to enter the channel.

Last night I observed an eclipse of the moon.

Wednesday, 24 September

God showed his mercy on the other two ships, and by his will the fleet was once again united. We sailed on to an island called Amona.

During this journey, Columbus's health broke down : he was exhausted both physically and mentally. Incapacitated by a severe fever, he lost both his sight and his memory. His plans to explore the Carib islands were abandoned by the crew, who preferred to sail for Isabela instead. On Monday, 29 September, the fleet arrived at Isabela. Although, by this time, Columbus was feeling a little stronger, it took him five more months to fully recover. He appointed his brother, Don Diego as Adelantado, with all the much envied privileges which went with that title.

Monday, 24 February 1495

I severely punished some of the cacique Guatigana's deputies for killing ten Christians and setting fire to a hut containing forty sick men. I ordered that the men be sent to Castile as prisoners.

It greatly saddens me to report that the Christians on Española are behaving despicably, and the Indians are refusing to obey them. The caciques are not united, and I propose to take advantage of their disunity to conquer the island and punish the Indians for killing the Christians.

Monday, 24 March

I ordered that two hundred infantry march from Isabela to attack the Indians with crossbows and harquebuses. After this, I instructed that twenty hounds and the cavalry of twenty horse be moved in. We played a splendid trick on the leading cacique, Caonabó, who is guilty of the murder of twenty Christians. We got him to try on a set of gorgeous looking brass fetters, from which there is no escape. Him and his brother shall be sent back to Spain, and his wives imprisoned.

Over the next year, Columbus reduced the Indians to obedience. He fixed how much cotton and gold they had to pay, and issued brass medals as proofs of payment. Five hundred Indian slaves were sent back to Castile under the command of Antonio de Torres, to be converted to the Christian faith.

Thursday, 10 March 1496

Having made peace in the island, and built three forts, I embarked at dawn for Spain, in order that I might give an account of all these events to your Majesties. I am taking with me two ships - Juan de Aguado being in command of the other - two hundred and twenty-five Christians and thirty Indians.

Wednesday, 6 April

Our provisions are running low, and my men are very tired and depressed. For the last year they have been eating a little wheat, rancid bacon, rotten cheese and a few beans and chick-peas, causing them to be very run down. I am steering a course for the Carib islands.

Saturday, 9 April

I lay anchor today at María Galante.

Sunday, 10 April

Although it is not the done thing to leave port on a Sunday, we cannot stand on ceremony, for we are too short of food.

As we were just about to land at Guadalupe, a crowd of women rushed out of the woods towards us. They carried bows and arrows, and had feathers on their heads. Their legs were bandaged from the calf to the knee so as to make them look thicker and more elegant. Instead of landing, we sent two Indians ashore. The women told us to go to their men on the northern islands who would barter food for our small trifles.

When we approached the women, they formed an ambush; but we soon frightened them with our crossbow shots, and they ran away. We looked inside their houses, which were square rather than round, and took only sufficient cassava bread for our needs. In one hut, we found a human hand roasting on a spit.

Monday, 11 April

The forty men I had sent on a reconnaissance expedition returned. One of the ten women they had taken prisoner was a cacique's wife - though she is more like a mad dog - who had very nearly choked to death the Canary Islander who had brought her. As I did not want the women to bear any grudges against us, I sent them all back with presents.

Wednesday, 20 April

With fresh supplies of water, bread and wood, I set sail at last from Guadalupe. I hope to make great progress in these calm conditions.

Friday, 20 May

We are in ever greater need of provisions, the daily ration now being just six ounces of bread and a pint and a half of water. My pilots are uncertain of our whereabouts, but I am convinced from my compasses that we are just to the west of the Azores.

Sunday, 22 May

I found out today that we are indeed one hundred leagues off the Azores.

Tuesday, 7 June

Tonight I ordered that the sails be taken in, fearing that we might strike land at Cape St Vincent. Few of the crew - a pessimistic lot at the best of times - share my confidence, and some of them are suggesting that we throw the Indians over-board so as to save on provisions. This I have most firmly forbidden.

Wednesday, 8 June

The pilots were still totally bewildered about where we were - some believing we were near England, others thinking we were near Galicia when, God be praised, we caught sight of Odemira which lies between Lisbon and Cape St Vincent.

Saturday, 11 June

Our two ships finally lay anchor in Cádiz harbour.

Summary chart of important events in the Second Voyage

25 September 1493	The fleet of seventeen ships left Cádiz
7 November	A party of eight men under Márquez went missing
14 November	Attacked by a canoe off San Juan Bautista [Puerto Rico]
22 November	Two Spaniards were found murdered at Monte Cristi
28 November	News reached the fleet that Navidad had been burnt down
11 December 1493- 12 March 1494	Columbus was ill and did not keep a journal
12 March	He left Isabela for the gold mines of the Cibao
9 April	Hojeda was sent to Santo Tomás to relieve Margarit
29 April	Columbus crossed to Juana [Cuba]
6 May	He anchored off Jamaica
30 June	His ship ran aground on his return to Jamaica
20 August	He reached Española
24 September	Columbus's health broke down
24 February 1495	Guatigana's men were imprisoned for killing ten Christians
24 March	The infantry and cavalry advanced from Isabela to attack the Indians. This was the beginning of the programme of subjugation
10 March 1496	Columbus began his return journey to Spain
10 April	The Spanish were attacked by Carib women at Guadalupe
11 June	The fleet returned to Cádiz

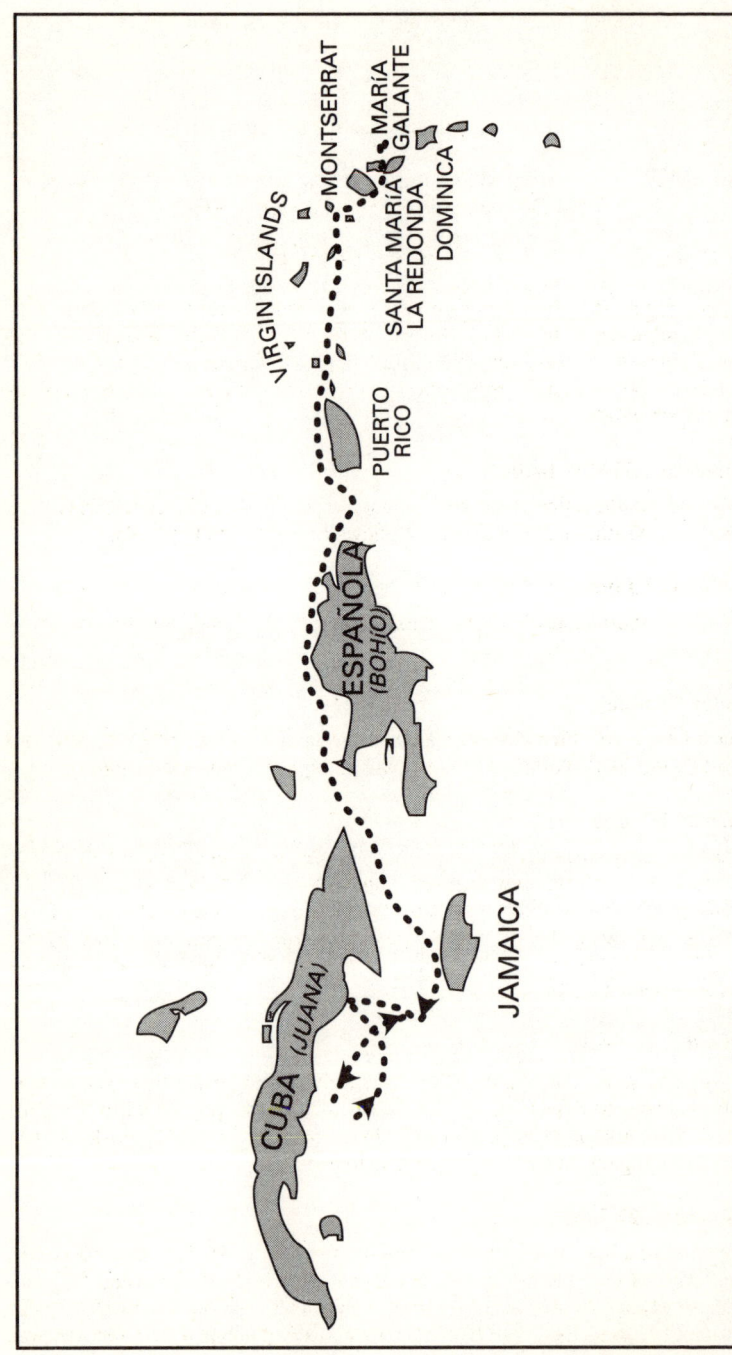

18. The route of Columbus's Second Voyage, 1493-6

Chapter VII

The Third Voyage, 1498-1500 :
The Return in Chains

Anxious about the well-being of the settlers we had left, I resolved to return to the Indies straight away. Instead, it took me almost a year before I got the two extra ships I wanted. These I sent off in advance of the others in February 1497. Neglect and poor management meant that it was a further year until the rest of my fleet was fitted out.

Wednesday, 30 May 1498

We set sail, in the name of the Holy Trinity, from the port of San Lúcar. Our six vessels carried sufficient provisions to relieve the settlers on Española.

Thursday, 7 June

Arriving at the island of Porto Santo, we heard Mass and took on water and wood.

Sunday 10 June

After a journey of three days, we reached Madeira where we were warmly welcomed by the captain of the island. We also took aboard more provisions.

Tuesday, 19 June

We arrived at Gomera in time to witness a French warship attempting to capture two Spanish vessels. On our approach it quickly made off. When I realised what was happening, I sent three ships after them. One of the captured ships they let go; as for the other, the six Spanish on board easily overcame the four French crew. When they returned to port, I agreed that the Frenchmen be exchanged for six natives which the French had carried away.

Thursday, 21 June

I set my course for the island of Ferro. On arrival there, I sent three ships under joint command to Española. The remainder of the fleet proceeded to the Cape Verdes. I am suffering severe gout pains in my leg and am very feverish. Despite this, I am doing my best to keep my log up to date.

Wednesday, 27 June

I anchored in a bay on the western shore of the island of Boa Vista, a miserable, barren place if ever there was one. The lepers, who come to the island for treatment, are always excited at the sight of a ship, and came to the shore to speak with us. They explained that the temperate climate, combined with the practices of eating turtle meat and smearing themselves in turtles' blood, helped to relieve leprosy. The turtles can be found in great abundance along the shore during the summer months. At night, the inhabitants patrol the beach with candles. When they find turtle tracks they follow them, turning all the turtles they discover on to their backs, and then returning the next morning to capture the largest turtles and let the smaller ones go. Meanwhile, the island's governors seem to spend almost their whole time killing mountain goats and salting them.

Sunday, 1 July

We reached the island of Santiago. Laying anchor near a church, I sent some men ashore to buy bulls and cows to take to Española. It is an unhealthy, sickly spot this, and I am determined to spend only a short while here.

Thursday, 5 July

We left the island of Santiago, sailing on a south-westerly course, but have made little progress in the strong currents.

As the fleet approached within five leagues of the Equator, it grew so hot that the sailors feared they should be burnt alive. The intense heat lasted for more than a week, scorching the wheat, and bursting open casks of wine and water. Eventually, the weather became cooler, wet and misty; and a favourable east wind came to the sailors' rescue.

Tuesday, 31 July

Desperate for water and with our provisions going bad, I resolved to sail for Española to check that there was no disorder amongst the people we had left there. At midday, land was sighted some fifteen leagues away, and we prayed to God for safe deliverance. Our Lord showed us three mountains lying all together on an island, to which I gave the name Trinidad. We cruised along the southern shore and anchored near Cape Galera. The land is as green as the orchards of Valencia in April.

Wednesday, 1 August

Anchoring at Punta de la Playa, my men went ashore excitedly and found water from a brook. Some fishermen had left their tackle on the beach and run off. We also found some footprints of goats and small monkeys.

We continued along the coast of this lovely, wooded isle, aided all the while by the westward-flowing current.

Thursday, 2 August

We were proceding to Punta del Arenal, hoping to repair the ships and obtain provisions, when suddenly we noticed a large canoe with twenty-five armed Indians following us. They had lighter skins than those on the other islands, and wore their hair long, like women. They stopped at about a lombard shot away and began to shout at us. We could not understand what they were saying but coaxed them nearer by holding up brass pots and mirrors. To show our good will, I then ordered that one of my men play a pipe and bang a tambourine; that another sing and play a kettle-drum; and that some of the young lads dance. All this carried on for two hours. But far from having the desired effect, the Indians thought that my men were doing a war dance and began to shoot arrows at them, forcing them to retaliate. Unable to retreat, they paddled over, and one of my pilots greatly pleased them by going down into their canoe and giving them a hat and coat, along with some other trifles. In return, they promised that if we came ashore they would give us bread. However, when we arrived at Punta del Arenal, there was not a soul to be seen.

Friday, 3 August

We discovered some wells dug in the sand, containing very fine drinking water. While at anchor, we encountered a terrifying wave as tall as a mountain which snapped one ship's cable and swept it from its anchorage. I steered a course through the Boca del Dragón [Mouth of the Dragon] where the water gushes out to sea with all fury around the island of Paria.

Monday, 6 August

We have continued up the coast of Paria. On the shore were many Indians who came up to us in their canoes wishing to barter. They wear a cloth over their head and another over their genitals; apart from the women who, like those on Trinidad, go about completely nude. To find out more about this land - which I named Isla de Gracia - I ordered that six Indians be taken aboard. I was especially interested in the small gold mirror which each wore around his neck. They told me that the gold came from islands to the west, inhabited by cannibals. The women wore beautiful pearl bracelets around their arms which they said came from local oyster shells. I bartered for some of these pearls, so that I may take them back to Spain. On going ashore, I found that the Indians of this place - which they call Paria - are lighter-skinned than elsewhere, and have shorter hair, similar to that worn in Spain. Everyone is most friendly and hospitable. As usual, I instructed my men to put up a large cross.

Saturday, 11 August

Finding it impossible to navigate my ship in these parts - the depth of the water being less than three fathoms - I have spent several days at anchor along the coast. A small caravel which I had sent out to see if there was a passage between the islands, returned today, and from the information given to me by its pilot, I have concluded that all the land which I had at first thought to be islands, is really one long stretch of mainland, containing river mouths and bays.

Monday, 13 August

I steered a westward course along the northern coast of Paria, thanking God all the while for leading us safely towards new lands full of friendly people and riches.

Wednesday, 15 August

I left the Cape de Conchas to my south and the island of Margarita to my west, and steered due north-west in a sea full of oysters. Keeping watch for such long periods has made my eyes bloodshot.

Monday, 20 August

Anchoring between Beata Island and Española, I sent out a group of Indians to tell my brother, Bartolomeo, of our safe arrival.

Thursday, 30 August

Anxious that we might run out of provisions, I anchored at Santo Domingo, which city my brother has named after my father, Domenico. To my surprise, there is no sign whatsoever of the three ships I sent to Española when I was in the Canary Islands. I had hoped to rest here, but to my horror the whole place is in chaos. It seems that after we had left in March 1496, food shortage and disease amongst the men had led to a rebellion against my brother. The ringleader was the mayor, Francisco Roldán. He claimed that my brother had been ruling too harshly and greedily, and had encouraged the Indians not to pay their gold tribute. From what I hear, Roldán has been taking even more tribute from them, and has been imposing floggings and imprisonment for even the most minor transgressions.

It was good to hear how the mens' spirits had picked up when my two advance ships arrived, bringing food and news of my safe return to Spain. However, I was shocked to hear that when the other ships I had sent from the Canary Islands arrived, far from the sailors aiding my brother, they actually became friendly with the rebels.

Saturday, 22 September

I resolved to do nothing to the rebels until they arrived back in Spain. Instead, I offered them food and free passage home if they wished it. I am also willing to offer Roldán a free pardon when he turns up.

Monday, 24 September

Roldán is a very stubborn and defiant man, and he was at first unwilling to make peace. Later, he agreed to negotiate, but only with Carvajal, one of the captains of the fleet I had sent from the Canaries, and a man who I am not entirely sure I can trust. Eventually, I let him go, to make what pact he could with Roldán; but Roldán was only willing to start negotiating after some Indians captured in the siege of Concepción had been released.

Monday, 15 October

I received a letter from Roldán today, in which he puts all the blame for the rebellion on my brother, the Adelantado. He went on to make some excessive and most insolent demands.

Tuesday, 16 October

I fear that I have less than seventy men to fight against the rebels, and only forty of these can honestly be relied upon. I decided to send Roldán a personal message saying that I was prepared to discuss any reasonable proposal.

Wednesday, 17 October

Another letter from Roldán and the rebels, saying that they had only deserted the Adelantado because he had threatened to murder them. They claimed that they were awaiting my arrival, expecting me to be proud of what they had done.

Thursday, 18 October

I have sent five ships back to Spain, with a full account of what has happened. The remaining three ships have been fitted out for the Adelantado's exploration of the mainland of Paria.

Sunday, 11 November

Sickened by Roldán's excessive demands, I have ordered that there be an amnesty. Anyone who wishes to return to Castile and who comes forward within the next thirty days, will have any arrears of pay made good and the right to free passage. Those who do not come forward can expect to receive the full force of the law.

Wednesday, 21 November

An agreement has been reached with Roldán and the rebels. They will be provided with two ships, fully equipped with provisions, for their return journey from Xaraguá to Castile. Before leaving, Roldán's men will have all their pay arrears made up and given the option of taking their women and children with them. They will also be permitted to take a quota of slaves home. To all those who do not wish to return to Castile, I shall grant land upon the island. My only misgiving is that by letting the rebels have these ships, I am preventing my brother, the Adelantado, from continuing to explore the mainland of Paria.

Saturday, 24 November

I set off for Isabela, leaving Don Diego in charge at Santo Domingo.

By the end of January 1499, the *Niña* and *Santa Cruz* were fitted out and ready to sail to Spain with the rebels. A fierce storm badly damaged the *Niña* and forced the ships to put into another port. Roldán's men were soon complaining that the repairs to the ships were taking too long, and that Columbus had deliberately caused the delays so as to spite them.

Thursday, 25 April 1499

Shipworms are now destroying our vessels, and provisions are going bad. Consequently, I have ordered that we return to Santo Domingo.

Tuesday, 21 May

I have written a curt letter to Roldán, urging him to obey your Majesties and to live in peace.

Saturday, 3 August

I have once again appealed to Roldán to see sense and abandon his ways. He agreed, on condition that fifteen of his men should be allowed to go directly to Castile; and those who stay should have houses and land. I am so concerned to put an end to this whole wretched affair that I have agreed to these conditions. I have also consented to restore Roldán to his former office of mayor. The dispute is now settled but I think it wise before leaving for Castile myself, to appoint a force to keep the peace and crush the slightest disorder. As part of their duties, these men will make sure that the Indians pay tribute.

Sunday, 29 September

Alonso de Hojeda arrived on Española. He had been exploring the coast of Paria when twenty of his men had been wounded by Indians. He claimed that shortage of supplies had driven him here.

Thursday, 26 December

A dismal day indeed, during the course of which I was attacked by a group of Indians and disloyal Christians, as if I were nothing better than a Moor. In fear of my life, I took to sea in a small caravel. The Lord said to me 'Oh, man of little faith, fear not I am with you'; and with that he scattered my enemies.

Monday, 3 February 1500

I set out for Santo Domingo, intending that after this I should make for Castile and tell your Highnesses everything that has happened.

Leaving Roldán behind, Hojeda sailed for Xaraguá, the very home of Roldán's rebels. When he heard that Columbus had not yet paid them their wages due, Hojeda offered to lead them to Santo Domingo so as to force Columbus to pay up. Many followed Hojeda, and those who refused to do so were beaten up. The rebels then prepared to attack Roldán who they viewed as a traitor seeing as he was now in Columbus's service. News of their plans leaked, however, and Roldán was able to assemble a strong force to crush Hojeda, who had to retreat. His position was further improved in June when a plot to kill him was thwarted, and he managed to capture Don Hernando and some of the other rebels.

Meanwhile, charges of cruelty and inability to govern continued to be levelled against Columbus and his brothers. The first formal written complaints were also sent to the King and Queen of Spain.

While Columbus was in Concepción dealing with the rebels at the end of August 1500, Francisco de Bobadilla arrived at Santo Domingo.

Columbus had certainly requested that Spain should send someone out to witness what the rebels were doing; but it soon became clear that Bobadilla had been sent out to determine whether Columbus was guilty of the accusations which the rebels were making. If this was the case, he had been empowered to take over as governor.

Columbus maintained that Bobadilla only listened to the rebels and to Bishop Fonseca who in any case bore a grudge against him. In early October Columbus and his brothers were arrested, clapped in chains and put on Andres Martín's ship. As they were taken aboard, horns were blown, and the rebels were even allowed to shout insults at Columbus and his brother. During the journey, Martín offered to remove the chains but Columbus, full of bitterness and pride, refused, arguing that as he had been placed in chains in the name of the King and Queen of Spain, he should wear them until they ordered them to be removed.

Friday, 20 November

I wrote to the King and Queen today to inform them officially that I had arrived in Cádiz.

19. Christopher and Bartholomew Columbus are arrested and enchained [by Theodor de Bry *Americae Pars Quarta* (1594)]

Thursday, 17 December

As soon as the King and Queen heard that I had returned in chains, they voiced their displeasure at what Bobadilla had done, and ordered that I be set free. They also requested that I come to Court at Granada.

At Granada, their Majesties received me affectionately, and promised me that all those guilty on Española would be punished by a new and wiser governor, Don Nicolás de Ovando, who would be despatched to Española immediately. Bobadilla was to restore my property, rights and privileges which he had so unjustly stripped me of.

Summary chart of important events in the Third Voyage

30 May 1498	The fleet of six vessels set sail from San Lúcar, bound for Española
19 June	The crew defeated a French attack at Gomera
21 June	Columbus was ill with gout and a fever
1 July	Bulls and cows were loaded aboard at Santiago to take to Española
	The crew experienced ferocious heat at the Equator and their provsions were ruined
31 July	Trinidad was discovered
2 August	A canoe carrying twenty-five Indians attacked the Christians off Punta del Arenal
6 August	Six Indians were captured off the coast of Paria
30 August	Columbus heard about Roldán's rebellion on Española
18 October	Five ships were sent back to Spain to give an account of the rebellion
21 November	The first of many broken agreements was reached with the rebels
February 1500	Hojeda and the rebels attacked Roldán but were forced to retreat
June	Another plot to kill Roldán was thwarted
August	Bobadilla arrived from Spain to investigate the rebels' accusations against Columbus and his brothers
October	Christopher and Diego Columbus were returned to Spain in chains
20 November	They arrived back in Cádiz
17 December	The King and Queen ordered that they be set free and be brought to Court at Granada

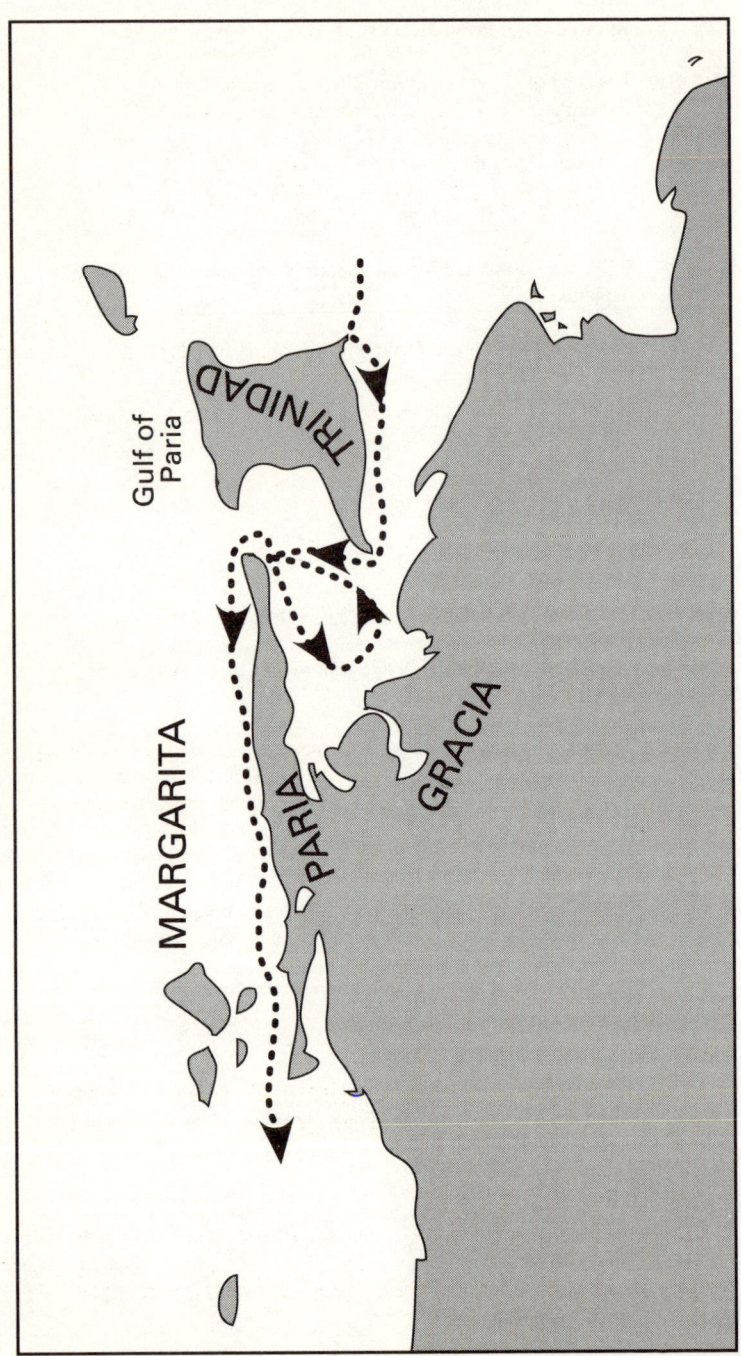

20. The route of Columbus's Third Voyage, 1498-1500

Chapter VIII

The Fourth Voyage, 1502-4 : 'The Voyage of Disasters'

'Very noble Señores:

... Our Almighty God has shown me the highest favour which, since David he has not shown to anybody... I am returning to the Indies in the name of the Holy Trinity and intend to come back. But being mortal, I leave to my son Don Diego the tenth part yearly of the total income which you will derive from there...'

Seville, 2 April 1502

.S.
S.A.S.
X.M.Y.
Xpo Ferens

Monday, 9 May 1502

With my rights and privileges now confirmed in writing by the King and Queen, I sailed with three other caravels from the harbour at Cádiz. I have persuaded my brother Bartolomeo, the Adelantado, to join the expedition, though he was very reluctant to do so.

Wednesday, 11 May

We have made almost no progress at all on account of the strong south westerly wind. Now that we are finally able to leave, I intend to first sail to Arcila on the coast of Africa to rescue the Portuguese from the hands of the rascally, infidel Moors.

Wednesday, 25 May

Finding that the Moors were no longer besieging Arcila, I steered a course for Maspalomas in the Grand Canary, where I have now taken on water and wood, and am ready to sail tonight for the Indies.

Wednesday, 15 June

The sea has been exceedingly rough and the wind very strong. However, with God's aid we arrived safely this morning at the island of Martininó [Martinique], where I propose staying a few days. I ordered that more water and wood be taken on board, and that the men wash their linen.

Friday, 24 June

One of my ships is proving very troublesome - not only is she slow, but the crew are finding it difficult to hoist her sails without capsizing her. If I get the chance, I intend to trade her in for a better one at Santo Domingo where - I hope it does not displease your Majesties - I must put down.

Thursday, 30 June

The sight of dolphins jumping out of the water signalled to me that a terrible storm was imminent. I sent ashore the captain of the *Gallega,* Pedro de Terreros, to request shelter for us, but he came back and reported that the new governor, Ovando, would not allow them to enter the port. Nor would he delay the departure of a treasure fleet bound for Castile under the command of my friend Antonio de Torres, but including the rebel Roldán and that scoundrel Bobadilla, both of whom had done me so much harm on my last voyage. Accordingly, I anchored as close as I could under the land. It seems scarcely credible that, in time of mortal danger, I, Viceroy and Governor-General of the islands and continent of Asia and the Indies, am being denied refuge in the very land that I have acquired for my home country.

Saturday, 2 July

The storm raged all day yesterday, and last night three ships were torn from their anchorages. The *Santo* lost the boat in which Captain Terreros had gone ashore. The *Santiago de Palos* - the caravel I want to trade for another - ran right out to sea, and water has run all over her deck. Each ship feared that the others were lost.

Sunday, 3 July

We compared notes on how each of us had weathered the storm. Whereas I had stayed close to shore, my brother, the Adelantado (experienced sailor though he be), had made the extraordinary decision to go out to sea. By God's saving grace, our ships - unlike those of the rebels - had been protected.

Today I witnessed an incredible sight : an enormous ray - which one of the sailors had harpooned - pulling a boat into the harbour at Azua, without oars.

Thursday, 14 July

There being no wind, we were at the mercy of the currents which carried us towards some small sandy islands near Jamaica. I have called these 'the Puddles' on account of the little pools of water found in the sand.

Sailing south, the fleet next came to the island of Guanaja, where Bartholomew Columbus went ashore with two boats. While the men were admiring the pine trees and the golden coloured earth, there arrived a canoe with twenty-five Indians - men, women and children - all with narrower foreheads than they had seen elsewhere. To the Spaniards they appeared as a wealthy and civilised people, giving them cotton shirts embroidered with different designs, shawls, large wooden swords and flint knives. They also had stocks of maize, wine and cacao beans which they used as currency. Columbus detained the oldest of them with a view to finding out more about the secrets of the land.

Postponing his departure for Cuba, he sailed instead towards Veragua in search of a way into the South Sea and the Land of Spices. The weather was terrible - incessant rain, thunder and lightning. At Caxinas Point - so named after a tree producing wrinkled olives - they were confronted by Indians wearing dyed shirts and breechclouts. In the skirmish that followed, the Spaniards were amazed to find that the Indians' cotton jerkins were sufficiently thick to protect them against their darts and even some blows from their swords.

On the east coast, the natives - whose skins were almost completely black - wore no clothes at all, and were adjudged wild and ugly. The Indian guide they had captured on Guanaja told them that these people were cannibals and pierced holes in their ears the size of hens' eggs. This is why Columbus came to name this stretch of coast the Costa de las Orejas.

Sunday, 14 August
Mass on shore today, conducted by the Adelantado. Attended by the captains and many of the crew.

Wednesday, 17 August
I ordered that boats be sent ashore, that we might formally take possession of the land in your Highnesses' name. More than a hundred Indians carried gifts of food which they presented to the Adelantado. In return, the Adelantado gave them the usual trifles. Even our interpreter, however, found it difficult to understand the Indians here.

Thursday, 18 August
More than two hundred natives came and brought more food - tasty chickens, geese, roast fish, and red and white beans. Though flat, this is a lovely land, full of pines and oaks, and with a wealth of animals - pumas, stags, roe deer and a variety of fish. Not all the Indians go naked here, some wearing sleeveless shirts. Many also have tattoos of animals - lions and deer - burnt into their arms. Some of those we saw have terrifying black and red stripes on their faces. Their foreheads do not seem to be as broad as on many of the other islands but some of them have large locks of hair hanging down, which made it difficult to judge. The more important people wore red or white head cloths. They speak many languages but do not appear to have a religion.

Thursday, 14 September
Having left Caxinas Point almost seventy days ago, we have by now covered some sixty leagues along the coast. We took care to anchor each night, being all

this time at the mercy of the winds. Today we reached a great cape where the wind and current were favourable, and which I have named Cape Gracias a Dios [Thank God Cape].

Saturday, 16 September

It pains me to have to report the loss of some of my men today. The circumstances surrounding this are as follows. When I launched the boats to take on water and wood, they made for what seemed like a deep river with good access. While they were down the river - El Río de Desastres, as I have come to call it - the wind increased, the sea became rougher, and one of the boats sunk, drowning all those who were in it.

Sunday, 25 September

We lay anchor at the island of Quiribirí, a delightful place indeed - the land being high, and full of rivers and palm trees. In the village of Cariay - surely not far from Cathay - we were confronted by a great many Indians bearing bows and arrows, clubs and palm-tree spears tipped with fish bone. At first these people felt threatened but when they realised that we meant them no harm, they swam out to our ships and were keen to trade their weapons, shirts and charms with us. Anxious not to show them that we were over-eager to seize their possessions, I ordered that presents be distributed to them but for some inexplicable reason, they merely gathered these together and left them by the landing point. We resisted their invitations to come ashore and passed the time instead in repairing the ships.

Wednesday, 28 September

The Indians sent out to us their most senior member, carrying a banner. He was accompanied by a girl of about eleven and another of about seven. Both were very showily dressed, and as shameless as if they were whores. The two girls were brought aboard, taken care of, clothed, fed and then returned. Strangely enough, they too returned all the things we had given them, as if they did not want to be under any obligation to us.

Thursday, 29 September

In the possession ceremony ashore today, the Adelantado took the opportunity of asking two leading men some questions but they were so terrified at the sight of pen and paper that they ran away.

Sunday, 2 October

The Adelantado has found some tombs and carved tablets in a large wooden palace. He noted three bodies, perfectly preserved in cotton cloth and without giving off the faintest trace of smell.

I took two leading Indians to act as guides down the coast - these Indians being surely the most intelligent that we have ever come across.

I was told of a remarkable land called Ciguare, where the people go about clothed and live not in huts but in houses. Furthermore, they have horses, and for their weapons have swords, bows and arrows, and cannon on their ships.

Monday, 3 October

Mistakenly thinking that I had kidnapped the two men from yesterday, a group of Indians came down to the shore, and four came on board to offer a ransom. They also brought two small wild boars as presents but I ordered that they be paid for them. Later, a crossbowman brought along what appeared to be an enormous polecat but with the face of a man. It was so viscious that we had to cut off an arm and a leg. One of the boars - so aggressive up until this time - backed off at the sight of it. I then asked that the boar and the cat be thrown together, where-upon the cat seized the boar by the neck and bit him until he squealed in agony.

Wednesday, 5 October

I set a course for Cerabaró Bay, navigating between the islands which were so close on either side that the branches of trees brushed against the ships. On one of these islands we found twenty canoes, and Indians who wear nothing other than a gold mirror or eagle around their neck. One of these mirrors they traded for three hawks' bells. They said that the gold lay not far away on the mainland.

Friday, 7 October

Now on the mainland, the Indians irritatingly refuse to sell any mirrors to us. I ordered that two of their number be seized, with a view to learning more about these people. They say that much gold can be found not far from here, and named a few places, all of which I made a careful note of.

Thursday, 20 October

Near the river Guayga, we were confronted by over a hundred Indians who rushed into the water, brandishing their spears, beating a drum and blowing horns. When closer, they started to squirt towards us a peculiar juice from a herb which they were chewing. My men were soon successful in pacifying them, after which exchanges of mirrors for hawks' bells began.

Friday, 21 October

The Indians hid behind shelters and would not come out for a long while. I ordered that my men should stay on the boats until they could be certain of a friendly reception. With this, the Indians started to yell, beat drums and sound horns; then they threatened to hurl spears at us if we came any closer. My men were so furious at this that one fired an arrow, wounding an Indian in the arm; and another fired a cannon which caused them to run away in terror. After this, there was peace but very little trading went on because the Indians had come pre-pared for war.

At Cateba we saw a king who protected himself from the torrential rain with a huge leaf. Nearby was some sort of building which seemed to have been made from stone and lime. I took care to order that a piece be taken back to Spain as a souvenir.

Wednesday, 2 November

Today we entered a harbour, full of little vessels and so beautiful that I have called it Puerto Bello [Panama]. I propose to shelter here from the impending storm, and then to continue to look for that strait leading to the South Sea and the Lands of Spices.

Thursday, 10 November

We have reached a harbour surrounded by maize fields. As we approached a canoe of Indians they all dived into the water, thinking that we were about to attack them.

Saturday, 26 November

We lay anchor in such a tiny harbour that it was probably only capable of holding five or six ships [Puerto Retrete]. The entrance to it was so narrow that any Indian wanting to attack could have done so with ease from the jagged rocks on either side. We spotted great lizards on the shore - capable of dragging off a man into the sea and eating him.

Saturday, 3 December

Seeing as the Indians were unwilling to respond to civil treatment and wish to fight instead, I was forced to have recourse to firing a cannon. They yelled back that it would take more than that to frighten them. So I ordered a second shot to teach them a lesson! The ball came down in the middle of a group of Indians on top of a hill. This put paid to their arrogance and disrespect!

Thursday, 8 December

The weather has been very unsettled these last few days. Sometimes the winds have taken us towards Veragua, at other times back to Puerto Bello again. The wind has frequently been accompanied by terrible thunder and fiery lightning. The rain has been so heavy that my men have been wet through for days on end and are in a very depressed state.

Tuesday, 13 December

We passed by an enormous waterspout which raises water up to the clouds in a thick column. If the sailors had not taken the precaution of reciting the Gospel, it would undoubtedly have swamped everything.

Friday, 16 December

Today we regained sight of the *Vizcaína* - lost for three days - though her boat is still missing.

Although the water is calmer, even now our troubles are not over, for we have been surrounded by sharks all day - a frightening experience indeed for my men, who were convinced that their presence is a bad omen. They have also heard that these monsters can seize a man's arm or leg in their teeth and cut it clean off with one bite of their saw-like teeth. We killed a number of these sharks with a chain hook, to which we attached a piece of red cloth, but they continued to pursue us. Extraordinarily enough, when we opened one of their bellies we found a huge turtle which was still alive and which we now have on deck. All the meat and fish we had brought from Spain having been consumed, and seeing as we are in a becalmed state, we are reduced either to eating the shark, or to take our chance with the damp biscuits, now full of worms. Some men are waiting until it is night so as not to see exactly how many worms there are in these biscuits.

Saturday, 17 December

Going ashore at Hulva, we found that the people here live in cabins in the tops of trees. Presumably, this is because they are afraid of the griffins which inhabit these parts.

Tuesday, 20 December

No sooner had we left this harbour than the wind rose up again, and has forced us to enter another harbour.

Friday, 23 December

Venturing out again, we experienced an even worse fate, with the wind blowing us back into the same harbour we were in earlier.

Tuesday, 3 January 1503

The *Gallega* now repaired, and with good supplies of maize, water and wood, I steered a course for Veragua. The winds were still unfavourable.

Friday, 6 January - the Feast of the Epiphany

The Lord has at last granted me a safe harbour. We anchored near the river which the Indians call Yebra and which I have renamed Belén. I then sent boats to where the Indians said the gold mines were.

Saturday, 7 January

The Indians were afraid to speak to us and were ready to defend themselves. Then the Indian who had travelled with us told the others that we meant them no harm. After this, trade began in gold mirrors, quills of gold dust and gold nuggets. The Indians made out that their gold was especially valuable because it came from distant, rugged mountains.

The bad weather has begun again.

Wednesday, 11 January

The King of Veragua, whom the Indians call the Quibián, spent an hour aboard my vessel, after which there was the usual exchange of gold for hawks' bells.

Tuesday, 24 January

The Río Belén has flooded without any warning whatsoever, the water striking us with such fury that it broke a cable and dashed us against the side of the *Gallega,* carrying her mizzen mast away.

The storm still rages, making any exploration quite impossible. In fact, both ships run the risk of sinking with all hands on board.

Monday, 6 February

I have sent seventy men into the interior. After beating their way against the rain, they found mines at a distance of five leagues. At the top of one hill it was pointed out to them how much gold there was in the surrounding regions; so that in a mere ten days a man might collect as much gold as a child could carry.

Thursday, 9 February

The men returned with some gold which they had gathered among the roots of trees, without the aid of any digging tools.

Friday, 17 February

Some men who returned to the ships reported how yesterday they had encountered a cacique - there are many in these parts - who chewed a dry herb, sometimes with another powder besides. His leading men also used it, though it rotted their teeth. The Adelantado and thirty men have continued to other villages in search of gold and to establish a new town.

Thursday, 30 March

I had hoped to depart for Spain before now; but we find ourselves trapped by half a fathom of sand which blocks the river mouth. On hearing a report that the cacique of this country (who they call the Quibián) plans to set fire to the houses we had built and kill the men, I ordered that he and all his advisers be taken prisoners and sent to Castile, and his people be made slaves.

Accordingly, the Adelantado set off today with seventy-four men for the village of Veragua.

Saturday, 1 April

The Adelantado returned - without having lost a single man killed or wounded - and was pleased to present me with gold mirrors, eagles and gold coronets.

I have prayed constantly for God to rescue us from our dire condition; and at times I have shown but too little faith. This Easter's Eve, however, God showed us his favour by sending heavy rain, making the waters sufficiently deep to get our ships out of the river mouth.

I resolved to leave Belén immediately, believing that if we stayed we may never be able to sail away. Accordingly, our three ships sailed for Santo Domingo, in the name of the Holy Trinity. Even now, the ships' keels caught on the sandy bottom. About a league outside the harbour, I sent a boat ashore for water and other provisions.

Tuesday, 11 April

There is still no news of what has happened to the boat I sent. In view of my diminished crew and the extra strain on those who remained, some of the Quibián's children and relations managed to escape from a hatch which we had not had time to secure. It grieves me that some of those who had not escaped have hanged themselves from the deck beams, bending their knees to avoid their feet touching the deck.

The garrison ashore begged me to take them away from their hopeless situation and the constant attacks from the Indians; and I agreed that as soon as the weather improved I should take them aboard.

Thursday, 20 April

Yesterday and today the garrison have been using their boat to transport themselves and their equipment on board, there being nothing left on shore apart from the hulk of the *Gallega*.

And so we set sail, first along the coast and then on a course for Española. My men mistakenly thought that we should steer due north at once, believing that I intended to take them all the way back to Spain in these poor ships and without adequate supplies!

At Puerto Bello we were forced to abandon the caravel *Vizcaína* which was leaking badly and riddled with more holes than a honeycomb. This leaves us with just two of our original four ships.

Wednesday, 10 May

Two very small islands have been sighted, full of turtles - like the entire sea in these parts.

Saturday, 13 May

We reached a cluster of small islands in the vicinity of Cathay [Cuba]. Here we lay anchor, my men completely exhausted with pumping out water the whole time, and having nothing to put in their bellies but a little biscuit, oil and vinegar.

Sunday, 14 May

A terrible storm has raged all night long. The sea is so rough, so covered with foam. Never did the heavens appear more terrible. Flashes of lightning occurred with such terrifying fury that we thought all the vessels were being consumed. The *Santiago de Palos* has damaged her stern and lost all her cables. The winds being easterly, it is impossible to make for Española, and I have resolved to steer towards Jamaica instead. The whole day was spent in manning the pumps again. We even resorted to using pots and kettles.

Thursday, 22 June - Eve of St John's Day

The water has risen so high in our ship that it is almost up to the level of the deck.

Friday, 23 June - St John's Day

We thankfully lay anchor in a safe harbour [Puerto Bueno] along the coast of Jamaica. There is no water as there is no village nearby.

Saturday, 24 June

We sailed eastward to our harbour at Santa Gloria, and shored up the ships. We
then built cabins on the ship to protect ourselves from the Indians. Before long,
the Indians - who, as it turned out, proved kind and friendly enough - came up in
their canoes ready to barter provisions. I thought it prudent to appoint two men to
check that there was fair trading : strings of yellow and green beads, red caps and
pairs of scissors were swapped for cassava bread.

God had indeed showed his special favour on us by leading us to this well-popu-
lated island, full of good things to eat. I decided to eat on board rather than
ashore, and gave my men strict orders to stay on the ship unless they had my
express permission to leave it.

I resolved to send messengers to Española, with word that I had too poor a vessel
to return to Castile, and needed a rescue ship with provisions and ammunition.

Friday, 7 July

I ordered that Diego Méndez de Segura, chief clerk of the fleet, and Bartolomeo
Fieschi, a gentleman from Genoa, set sail in two Indian canoes with a crew of six
Christians and ten Indian paddlers each. Méndez should then go on to Santo
Domingo while Fieschi should return to Jamaica to report his safe arrival. The
Indians brought with them flasks of water and cassava bread; the Christians
brought swords and shields.

Tuesday, 2 January 1504

What with them having nothing to eat and their extreme fatigue, many of my men
are now sick. Their eyes are sore and their teeth are rotting. In this depressed
state, with no news as to whether the canoes had ever reached Española, they
have begun to question my judgement and authority. For my part, the gout troubles me greatly. I am confined to bed and therefore unable to superintend the
actions of my men.

Francisco Porras (Captain of the *Santiago de Palos)* and his brother (the
Comptroller of the Fleet), burst into my cabin, fully armed, and complained in a
most insolent manner that I hadn't the slightest intention of leading them back to
Castile. I answered that I was just as keen to get home as they were; but the fact is
that we have no ship. Not really listening to a word I said, Porras turned his back
and shouted out to his men to join him. Some fifty men then ran around in complete confusion, shouting 'To Castile!' All this time, I was really in no state to be
on deck, and my advisers urged me to return below. The mutineers, who included
amongst their number one Bernal, an apothecary, then took possession of ten
Indian canoes. Others, who were anxious about being left on their own, also piled
in. I don't doubt that they will cause trouble for me in the lands they pass
through.

Before long, the Indians began to be influenced by the mutineers: they started to
bring us less food and charge us more dearly for it than before. They are commit-

ting outrages of robbery and violence on the Indians, and have killed some who were in their boat.

Monday, 26 February 1504

God has suggested to me a way by which we might obtain as much food as we want. I know from Müller's Astronomic Calendar that in three days time there will be a complete eclipse of the moon at midnight. Accordingly, I despatched one of the Indians who had accompanied us from Española, to gather all the principal men to come to a feast. When they arrived, I told them that his God intended to punish the Indians for not providing us with all the food that they should, and that he would soon send us a sign of his displeasure - the moon would disappear from the sky forever.

Thursday, 29 February

Tonight all the Indians watched with disbelief as the moon rose and gradually watched a shadow obscure its face. At first astonished, then terrified, the Indians prayed and prayed that God should forgive them, and that they would give the Christians everything which they wanted. On hearing this, I retired to my cabin, and when I knew that the moon would soon reappear, I came out and told them that God had now forgiven them and that shortly he would bring the moon back. Soon after this, they saw that what I had said was indeed coming true. From now onwards, they will not dare but give us all the food we ask for. It is incredible to think that they had not the remotest idea why the eclipse was going on.

There was still no news of Méndez or Fieschi. We are very anxious about them, thinking that they might have drowned or been killed by the Indians. If they have reached Española, then why hasn't Ovando sent me the ships which I need?

Saturday, 30 March

Fortune greatly favoured us today when a small ship arrived from Lares in Española, carrying a barrel of wine and some salt pork. The men were greatly relieved. I was given a letter from Méndez, giving details of what had happened on his voyage, and am now greatly reassured. His men seem to have been badly let down by the Indians who consumed all the drinking water on board - so necessary in this extreme heat. One of the Indians died of thirst, and others were far too weak to paddle. He explained how they even had to drink sea water. When they eventually reached Española, Mendez obtained a ship, which he supplied with provisions and sent to Jamaica. Then he had taken another ship himself for Spain.

I immediately made it known to the mutineers that Méndez had safely returned, and as further proof sent them a portion of salt pork. I also offered them safe-conduct and a pardon. All this they rejected, and if anything they became more contrary in their ways.

Sunday, 19 May

I sent out my brother, Bartolomeo, with fifty armed men to bring them to their senses. When they reached the mutineers on a hilltop above Santa Gloria they were greeted with contempt. By God's will, we killed five or six of them, after which the remainder ran away. Captain Porras and other prisoners were brought back; but my brother, the Adelantado, was wounded in the hand, and my chief waiter died from a lance stroke in his side. The rebels received more severe injuries - some on the shoulder, others on their arms, thighs and soles of their feet.

Monday, 20 May

Seeing that they were repentant, I granted the remaining mutineers a pardon. I am, nevertheless, keeping Captain Porras (and his brother) as prisoner, in case he should think of organising another rebellion. I have ordered that the men should be kept on the island until more ships arrive, there being too little room and insufficient rations for them on board.

Friday, 28 June

The ships I was expecting arrived from Santo Domingo. We set sail, with both mutineers and loyalists on board. Never in my life had I known so joyful a day. After being marooned for more than a year, we know at last that we are going home.

Tuesday, 13 August

We put in at Jamaica, having experienced great difficulties on account of contrary winds and currents. We were received hospitably enough and I was lodged in governor Ovando's house. What dismayed me, however, was that he released Porras - the ringleader - no doubt so as to undermine my authority and assert his own.

Thursday, 12 September

Shortly after setting sail from Santo Domingo, the main mast of one of our two ships split, and had to be sent back.

Later we experienced a terrible storm.

Saturday, 19 October

The mainmast broke into four pieces and I ordered that a replacement be made out of a lateen yard. I was forced to stay in bed, suffering badly from gout.

Thursday, 7 November

After a horrendous sea crossing, and with our foremast completely broken, we eventually arrived back at San Lúcar, from where I was brought to Seville, riddled by gout.

It irks me that having sweated so much blood and served their Majesties with such diligence and love, I have not been invited to Court.

Columbus lived in Seville with his brother for the next six months, both of them sick men.

May 1505

I set off for the Court of King Ferdinand where I learnt, alas, that the good Queen had died less than three weeks after I had returned from my voyage. Although the King received me courteously enough, he was really intent on taking away my rights and privileges. He had always had reservations about my project and he now seemed to begrudge the large share I had of the Indies.

On Ascension Day, 20 May 1506, just a day after making his last will, Columbus died in Valladolid. He was fifty-four years old, though his grey hair and haggard looks may have easily been taken for those of a much older man. His body was carried to Seville and buried in the Cathedral. King Ferdinand ordered that the memorial stone over his tomb read: 'To Castile and Leon, Columbus gave a New World'.

Columbus had not discovered a route to the Indies, as he had intended, and he died a disappointed man; but he had paved the way for the permanent European settlement of the New World. To contemporaries, however, even this was very far from clear. Believing that Amerigo Vespucci - the Florentine who had certainly helped prepare ships for Columbus's second and third voyages - was the first European to reach the New World when he landed on the Venezuelan Coast in 1499, a German mapmaker, Martin Waldseemüller, proceeded to make the momentous decision of naming the continent America.

Summary chart of important events in the Fourth Voyage

9 May 1502	Columbus's fleet of four caravels sailed from Cádiz
24 June	One of the ships was already proving unseaworthy
30 June	Ovando refused to allow the fleet to enter port at Santo Domingo
2 July	A fierce storm tore three ships from their anchorages
17 August	Columbus took possession of Veragua [Panama]
16 September	A ship's boat sunk off Cape Gracias a Dios, drowning all on board
25 September	The natives of the island of Quiribirí returned every present they were given
20 October	The crew were attacked by about a hundred Indians near the river Guayga
2 November	Columbus reached Puerto Bello, which he proposed to use as a base to search for the South Sea
13 December	The crew were terrified by an enormous waterspout
16 December	They continued through shark-infested waters
24 January 1503	The river Belén flooded, badly damaging the ships
30 March	A cacique and his advisers were taken prisoner but the fleet found themselves marooned at Veragua
11 April	Some of the prisoners managed to escape
20 April	At Puerto Bello the *Vizcaína* had to be abandoned
14 May	The fleet confronted a terrible storm off Cuba
7 July	Messengers were sent to Española for help
2 January 1504	Francisco de Porras's mutiny
29 February	Columbus tricked the Indians with an eclipse of the moon
19 May	Bartolomeo Columbus was wounded at Santa Gloria
13 August	Ovando released the rebel Porras against Columbus's will
7 November	The fleet, now just two ships, limped into San Lúcar

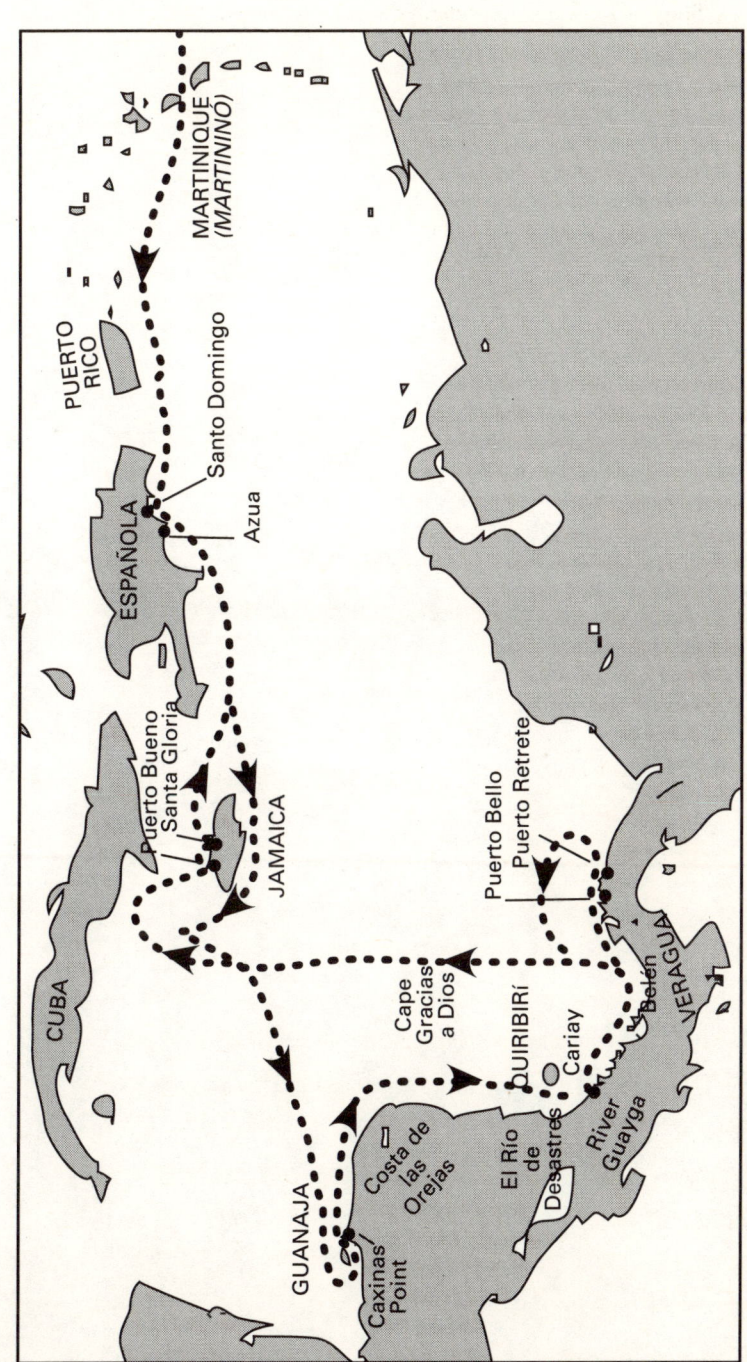

21. The route of Columbus's Fourth Voyage, 1502-4

Christopher Columbus

Chapter IX

The American Natives and Columbus

Too often, the 'primitive' natives are seen solely from the standpoint of the European conquerors. This chapter explores the reactions of the Indians to the strangers who came to their shores in 1492.

As dawn broke on the horizon, the Indians caught sight of what at first seemed to them to be mysterious canoes. As they drew nearer, though, they appeared so large that they looked more like floating houses. Many Indians took flight to the woods; but later their curiosity generally got the better of them and they came and offered the travellers casks of water and cassava bread.

The natives stared in amazement at these men, the like of whom they had never seen before. Their bodies seemed to be covered in a variety of strange colours and textures which appeared to conceal a human form; but all wore thick leather over their lower legs, hiding their feet. The Indians wondered how they managed to move easily, and run away from danger. Were these outer skins? Could they be removed? Imagine how hot it must be to wear these all the time! Why didn't they wear a white tunic, as some of their neighbouring islanders did?

There was something magical about the gifts they carried in their hands - wonderful trinkets and little toys. The Indians wondered where the strangers had come from - the skies, perhaps? Were these, then, gifts from the gods? In that case, their floating houses must have flown down from the sky where these people must live. The natives brought food and drink to honour the men from the sky; they knelt down before them, and the women kissed their feet in awe. In return, the Indians were given small, rounded pieces of metal (smaller than a bean), and with strange designs carved on them. These, the Europeans apparently exchanged for each others' goods - there being no bartering. These metal fragments had a picture of a man and a woman on them, looking at each other, each head wearing a crown. No doubt these must be the heavenly rulers themselves.

Others had a different reaction, believing the sailors in their boats to be monsters which had come up from the depths of the sea during the night. The brisk movement of the sails in the breeze was, for them, the monster flapping its wings, ready to make off. Their friends disagreed, fearing that the visitors were really cannibals, like the dreaded Caribs who periodically raided their shores; and their fears were only allayed when an Indian came forward to greet them, and explained how all the time he had been a guide for the strangers they had not mistreated him.

Some of these travellers had the most peculiarly coloured hair - not black but different hues, ranging from silver, through golden corn to dull earth. These men looked very strange - a combination of a shining, bald head and a hairy lower jaw, with a thin line of whiskers above their lips. The Indians touched these protruding hairs, as if there was something magical about them. Over all, the visitors were physically disappointing, with their big bellies, curiously narrow foreheads and their pale, bleached and unhealthy-looking skins. Not having a trace of paint on them, their faces seemed like white masks.

Only one man, taller than most of the others, stood out from the rest. He was dressed in unusual metal clothing, and wore a magnificent crimson cloth draped over his shoulders - but, oddly, no feathers. He had to be the chief - but then why did he not wear a crown like an Indian cacique? As soon as he landed, the tall man fell upon his knees, and started to utter mysterious sounds - presumably some sort of magical spell. As the Indians continued to watch in disbelief, another man came forward. First he dipped the end of a bird's feather into some peculiar black juice; and then he scratched the feather on a sheet of white material. With that, all the other men followed suit, as if they were taking part in a ritual!

The magic continued. A wooden cross - a shape of no significance to the Indians - was planted on a nearby hillock. Spellbound during the whole of these proceedings, they began to imitate the Spaniards' unusual chanting noises. Becoming more and more drawn into the mystery of the occasion, they allowed one of the strangers, dressed in a long black gown and wearing a rather strange black hat, to dip his fingers in a bowl of water and make the same cross sign on their foreheads. Next they were given pictures of a strangely dressed woman to wear around their necks. What were these - some sort of magic talismans? And if so, what did they protect them against? If they accepted them, did they run the risk of being enchanted? As the sun set, the visitors began to sing what they called the *Ave Maria* and the *Salve Regina*; amazing indeed that they knew two languages - one for speaking in, and another for this mournful chanting.

What next caught the natives' eye were the glistening wooden sticks which hung down from the sailors' left thighs - magic wands in special cases, perhaps? But no, for when one of the Spaniards unsheathed his sword, an Indian grabbed it by the blade, and badly cut himself. A great laugh went up from the sailors, who seemed on many occasions to be amused by the misfortunes and accidents of others. Suddenly, there was a flash and a cloud of smoke. One of the crew had let off a heavy lombard cannon. It caused great havoc and confusion amongst the Indians. Terrified, they fell to the ground, as if they had been struck by a thunderbolt. The Indians had only been used to bows and arrows, wooden spears,

22. Columbus's men plant a cross on Española, 6 December 1492
  [from Theodor de Bry *Americae Pars Quarta* (1594)]

clubs and poisoned darts; but they could not realise as yet what a deadly
weapon of destruction they had come up against.

When the sailors went on to claim possession of the new lands, their
actions were quite beyond the comprehension of the Indians. Personal
possessions were unknown to them; so they were puzzled by the sailors'
obsession to find gold. When the Spanish entered their huts, they quickly
lost interest when they found no gold, and moved on impatiently. The
Indians could attach no such value to the metal; to them it was just an

ornament, and copper was equally as valuable. Also, the strangers took great interest in the Indians' parrots, less for their beautiful plummage than for their squarking which, for some reason, sent them into roars of laughter. After many months at sea, the sailors' interest in their women was more understandable. Despite the fact that there was common ownership, this sharing of property among the Indians did not extend to their women folk. For, with the exception of the caciques (who had several wives) most of the Indian men spent their entire lives with just one woman. The Spanish attempt to capture some of their women horrified them.

These ruffians did not seem to have anything like the respect for their leader that the Indians had for their caciques - indeed, they sometimes openly defied his orders. As for the leader himself, it must be said that he did not set the best of examples - being frequently asleep in his cabin (they did not appreciate this was due to gout); whilst his men either staggered about, picking quarrels with one another, or were actually asleep - not in a hammock, but flat out on deck! At other times, these men rolled little cubes of wood across the deck, showing great excitement. They seemed a callous lot, taking pleasure once in cutting off a puma's leg, and then watching the injured animal fight against a boar.

When a cacique was invited to dinner on Columbus's ship, on the first voyage, the experience must have been novel to say the least: he is likely to have felt that a bulky, slow boat such as this would be hopeless to navigate between islands at sea, so only going to prove that these strangers had not come across the seas at all, but from the sky. On board, they were offered food, but being used to eating with their fingers, the Indians did not understand the purpose of the utensils that were put in their hands. They were also taken aback when they found that they were not allowed to take any of the food until all the Spanish had mumbled some kind of a chant. The cacique went on to sample only a small amount of food and drink; whereas the sheer quantity of food the sailors ate amazed him. What did he make of the rough Spanish wine that had slopped around at sea in a wooden cask for months; and the heavily salted provisions which they continued to prefer to what the natives offered them? Why were these men so unwilling to change their diet? Was it the diet which gave them their special powers?

In view of the great 'culture shock' which the Indians had experienced, it is surprising how quickly they adapted to the new ways. This may have been partly due to the fact that they had a strong desire to please the strangers who had troubled to visit their shores - even to the extent of urging them to stay longer. For, despite the ordeals they were subjected to, most Indians were prepared, initially at least, to welcome the Spanish.

Chapter X

The Legacy of the New World

'The discovery of America', declared the sixteenth century Spanish historian, Oviedo, 'was the greatest event in history since Hercules broke through the Straits of Gibraltar'. Others of Columbus's contemporaries regarded it as the eighth wonder of the world.

The sheer scale of the discovery can only be appreciated when we realise that the area of the Americas is roughly four times that of western Europe. The massive amount of knowledge accumulated gave a much more accurate conception of the world and an unprecedented widening of mental horizons. Columbus set the stage for a lengthy period of exploration by others, notably the Portuguese Ferdinand Magellan and the Spaniard Fernando Cortés. These voyages overturned the theory that the globe was mainly composed of land; indeed the oceans were now shown to cover more than two thirds of the entire surface.

The first legacy - food

When Columbus gathered the first plants to take back with him to Barcelona, little was he aware that he was ushering in a long period of gradual change in food. The movement of new crops and raw materials from the New World to the Old which he set in track fundamentally changed the flavour of food the world over and introduced the first *nouvelle cuisine*. Often bland and monotonous, the medieval menu greatly depended on salted and dried foods, such as mutton, salt pork and herring. Peasants' food was especially unappealing, consisting as it did of dark bread, cabbage, beans, pease pudding and cheese. The voyages of discovery had been stimulated partly by a demand for spices other than the familiar peppercorn and cloves. In this aim they were unsuccessful, but they did provide a huge range of new foods. Indeed it is no exaggeration to say that 'the American Indians are the main contributors to the world's varied cuisines today' [Jack Weatherford *Indian Givers* (Ballantine Books, 1988)]. Though the technique of barbecueing, first seen on Española, has caught on, the associated Indian practices of cannibalism and spider-eating have fortunately not.

Contact with America brought Europe face to face above all with the potato, where its subsequent introduction has been hailed as 'one of the major events in man's recent history' [R.N.Salaman *The History and Social Influence of the Potato (C. U. P.*, 1949)] . Specimens of sweet potato were brought back to the Spanish court by Columbus himself from the island of Haiti. The common potato did not arrive until about 1570. Nowhere in Central or North America was it cultivated before Columbus's time; but in South America an amazing three thousand varieties of wild potato were grown in the high altitudes of the Andes and the uplands of Colombia. As the land in both areas was unsuited to maize, the potato had become the staple crop. The Indian farmers even knew how to freeze potatoes by leaving them out on the high mountains at night in the freezing air. How the potato reached Europe is uncertain but it was probably exported from the Colombian port of Cartagena at the northern end of the Andes; the theory that it reached England from Virginia is certainly untrue, for the potato was never known in Virginia in the sixteenth or seventeenth century - so much for the popular English belief that Sir Walter Raleigh introduced it from his lands in Virginia!

Perhaps the most versatile of vegetables, the potato can be baked, boiled, fried and roasted, and even sliced into wafer-thin crisps. Before its introduction, Europeans had depended on wheat, rye, barley and oats as their staple diet; but they were subject to problems caused by weather, disease and birds. The potato, on the other hand, not only grows underground but grows more quickly and reliably than any grain, and can thrive in the cool, damp climate of northern Europe. In 1536, the Spanish conqueror of South America, Juan de Castellanos, described the potato as 'a gift very acceptable to the Indian, and a dainty dish even for the Spaniard'. Certainly Spaniards as well as natives were eating potatoes by 1620 in Peru and New Granada, and were starting to make potato flour, cakes and fritters. Others described potatoes as being 'no less tasty and agreeable to the palate than turnips themselves', and even as being as tender as a cooked chestnut, and with a better flavour, like a truffle. Its nourishing qualities were also recognised, especially for invalids. The Scottish philosopher, Adam Smith, in *The Wealth of Nations* (1776), described the potato as something 'from which the industrious poor derive an agreeable and wholesome variety of food'. It also made economic sense, for an acre of potatoes would produce a greater yield than an acre of wheat or rice, and was cheaper to produce.

Both the common potato and the sweet potato were also believed to be aphrodisiacs when cut into slices and swamped in a peppery sauce. In 1637 the English horticulturalist, John Goodyear, wrote that the potato has the effect of 'procuring lust and that with greediness'; and a contemporary of his claimed that it 'encrease Seed and provoke Lust' [Parkinson Herbal (1629)]. In Ireland, where the potato was first introduced in the late sixteenth century, it was believed to have some connection with the large size of their families. Meanwhile, potato juice was thought to be good for barrenness and impotence.

And yet, despite the advantages claimed for it, the potato was at first opposed in Europe before becoming generally accepted. Some people were suspicious for it broke with tradition, in that it grew from tubers rather than from seed. Then there was the flatulence it caused. Molière's *Bourgeois Gentilhomme* describes the whole experience of digesting a potato as 'somewhat windy'. The vegetable was also far from pleasing to the eye, having several differences to the potato today. It had particularly long roots, knobbly tubers with deep eyes, and bulbous growths which reminded people of the deformities of the hands and feet associated with leprosy. The Swiss thought that the potato caused scrofula; the Prussians that it caused rickets and consumption. In fact, as we know, the potato has several very healthy qualities, it being both a good source of vitamin C, which has helped to abolish scurvy, and of Bl, the anti-beriberi vitamin. Any resistance met by enthusiastic British landowners when they first introduced the potato to their tenants had been overcome by the end of the seventeenth century, when it ceased to be the preserve of the rich and was fast becoming a staple food. In Ireland, where the potato was ideally suited to the moist, cool atmosphere and the rich deep soils, the potato became such an important part of life that when the crop failed in the blight of 1846-47, the result was starvation.

Second only to the potato in terms of its impact on European diets has to be its close relative, the tomato. Probably brought from Mexico by Spanish priests in the mid sixteenth century, it was thought at first to be poisonous and was not widely accepted for another three hundred years, although we now know it to be rich in vitamins A and C. Until relatively recently, the tomato was much less attractive as a salad vegetable because of its misshapen appearance. It soon came to be called 'golden apple' because of its orangey-yellow colour; or 'love apple', on account of its alleged aphrodisiac qualities - a similar story to that of the potato. The tomato has revolutionised cooking, particularly perhaps in Italy. It is difficult to imagine a salad without this colourful addition; and it would be a strange pizza indeed which did not have its topping of tomatoes! In the western world, tomato soup, ketchup and juice continue to be great favourites. Today, the United States (notably California) still produces more tomatoes than any other nation.

Exotic peppers and chillies were also amongst the first items to go to Europe. Before Columbus's time, Europe only knew black pepper. Believing that he was near the Spice Islands, Columbus gave the name peppers to the orange, yellow, red and green bell-shaped vegetables with which the natives seemed to be flavouring their soup; but he found the taste disappointing, expecting something much more spicy. Not so with the chilli, which Columbus himself describes as 'a fruit as long as cinnamon, full of small grains as biting as pepper'. Chillies provided an excellent seasoning, and when pickled in vinegar, make tabasco. Cayenne pepper and paprika, on the other hand, are important ingredients in Indian curry and Hungarian goulash.

Life would be hard indeed for the chocoholic of today without the sensuous, silky texture of the chocolate bar. Botanists believe that the cacao ('bitter juice') tree, from which the bean is obtained, originated in the Amazon-Orinoco river basin. Long before Columbus, the Aztecs enjoyed drinking a mixture of cold chocolate, spices and pepper; they also used the bean as a unit of currency. The early sixteenth century explorer, Cortés, is said to have tasted his first drinking chocolate in a golden goblet, as a guest at Emperor Montezuma's palace. In 1528, Cortés returned from Mexico to Spain with cacao beans. It was not at all popular at first because the chocolate ('sour water') was found to be so bitter. Tradition has it that a group of nuns experimented by mixing it with hot milk and sugar. Suddenly it became popular to the European palate. No one had ever tasted anything quite like it before. By 1606, it had become popular in Italy, from where it spread to Austria, France and finally to England. London chocolate houses, the fore-runners of the gentlemen's clubs, became fashionable with the rich in the early eighteenth century. When processed to remove cacao oil, and mixed with vanilla, spices and (more recently) an emulsifier made from soya beans, it was found to be still more delicious. It was soon recognised as a good source of energy, and has won particular favour amongst people whose work requires physical endurance, such as athletes and the armed forces, who use it as an emergency ration. The small amount of caffeine in it also helps to stimulate the nervous system. (Another great source of caffeine, the coffee bean, was later taken to the New World and grown in large quantities in South America and the West Indies). Today, most of the world's cacao beans come from Brazil and West Africa; and Belgium, Switzerland, Britain and Germany are some of the biggest consumers of chocolate and chocolate-coated sweets.

Another product new to the Europeans was maize. Within half a century of the first voyages to the New World, maize (otherwise known as Indian corn), had become a familiar enough sight in Europe. The American Indians had developed over two hundred types of maize by the fifteenth century, which they boiled or ground into flour. When Columbus returned to Spain, he carried maize seeds from Cuba. Maize was soon introduced into Italy, Turkey, Portugal, France, Britain and Holland; and by the mid sixteenth century had reached China and Africa. It soon, however, lost much of its original popularity when those who adopted it found that their health deteriorated, on account of its lack of vitamin C. Although used today to make popcorn, it is mainly used for feeding livestock. The corn syrup, on the other hand, is much valued for making such things as ice-cream, cola, sweets and salad dressings, as well as, surprisingly, cosmetic blood used in films. Nevertheless, the true significance of maize lay in the way it was planted, rather than in the grain itself. The Indians did not simply scatter seed like the Europeans but planted carefully selected seed in pre-dug holes in the soil (see Plate

23.Indians sowing maize
[from Theodor de Bry *Americae Tertia Pars* (1591-2)]

[Highly efficient cultivation enabled the Indians to get three crops a year.
They laid the field out on a grid-shaped pattern, and carefully planted maize
seeds within a circle in each of the squares. The sheer size of the Indian maize
plantations astonished the Spaniards - Columbus's brother, Diego, claimed
that he walked eighteen miles through a field of maize, beans and squash.]

23). This was responsible for a major innovation in European farming,
eliminating wastage and thereby increasing the yield.

When Columbus 'raided the larder' of the New World he not merely
began the flow of potatoes, tomatoes, peppers, chocolate and corn, but a
huge range of other foodstuffs that Europeans take for granted in their
diets today. Rhubarb, as we have seen, was collected by Columbus's men
on the island of Amiga; then there was pineapple, excitedly described by
Columbus himself as 'a fruit in the shape of a pine cone, twice as big,
which fruit is excellent'. Other fruits which were discovered included the
gooseberry, the cranberry (soon the turkey arrived from Mexico to
accompany it), passion fruit and the blueberry. Amongst the vegetables,
Jerusalem artichokes, avocados, *zucchini* or *courgettes,* tapioca, and a
range of beans (kidney, butter, string, green and above all the perennial
favourite, the baked bean) were soon to be found on European tables.
Meanwhile, the sunflower provided an important new animal feed and
cooking oil. Peanuts and cashews have become not just great European
snack-foods this century but a major ingredient in meat and vegetable
dishes in China. Flavourings, such as vanilla and maple syrup also made

their appearance. The Indians had developed the practice of dipping fried bread into maple syrup - perhaps the origin of the doughnut. Even the apéritif Campari owes its popularity to America, the cascarilla bark used to flavour it coming from Samaná Cay, the actual place where Columbus first landed on 12th October, 1492.

Diets do, of course, take centuries to change, but Columbus's influence here should not be underestimated. His was the first contact that made these changes possible.

The second legacy - medicine and drugs

It has been estimated that perhaps two thirds of the medicines available in the world today have American Indian origins. As sophisticated pharmacists, the Indians were able to bring a great deal of expertise to western Europe, where medical standards throughout the middle ages were extremely primitive. Many cures were based on superstition and magic:

> 'For toothache: hang the beak of a magpie round your neck.
> For a headache: put goat's cheese on your head.
> For a fever: use a leech to suck blood from your arm.'

The Europeans took back with them a huge range of plants and barks. Bark containing quinine had been used for centuries by Amazon Indians to prevent and cure malaria. When it was introduced to Europe in c.1630, again for the treatment of malaria, it was expensive; but in the nineteenth century the active ingredient, called *ipecac,* was extracted, and quinine was used more generally in cases of dysentery. Until then, doctors in Europe had been using potions and leeches to treat a wide range of conditions. Today, quinine is an important ingredient of (Indian) tonic water, giving its distinctly bitter taste.

Other barks also had important medicinal qualities. Bark of poplar or willow was being used effectively by the Indians to cure headaches: the bark of another shrub, *Rhamnus purshiana,* is today the world's most commonly used laxative; juniper bark can be used as a salve on flesh wounds; whilst in 1535 the bark and needles of the Canadian evergreen Annedda were shown to have sufficient quantities of vitamin C to cure scurvy in as little as a week. Today, the popularity of herbal remedies owes much to the discoveries of this time.

In Mexico, the Aztecs' experience of human sacrifice had one good result - it made them masters of anatomy; the knives they used were sharp enough to cause minimal blood loss and few scars, as they adeptly lanced boils and removed tumours. Surgery in the Old World has been able to progress because of the discovery of *curare* in the Amazon in 1807. The effect of the drug is to relax the muscles sufficiently to put a tube into the windpipe during an operation. The isolation of the drug cocaine from the leaves of the Andean coca bush in the 1880's provided a useful anaesthetic for eye and dental surgery, although it has continued to be misused as well.

However, for all that was gained in medical knowledge from the New World, there was another result to be reckoned with - one which was to have devastating medical and social consequences. Syphilis was almost certainly brought back to Europe by Columbus on his first voyage in 1493. Having incubated in Spain and France, it spread to Italy, Germany, Britain, India, Russia, and even reaching China by 1505. Syphilis was then a more virulent and terrifying disease than it is now, and it often proved fatal. First, pustules formed on the genitals, the bones, eyes and nose became infected, and there was a great deal of muscular pain; but perhaps the mental effects were the most terrifying - incipient madness. There was no known cure, and syphilis continued to be a killer disease until the beginning of the present century when the chemotherapy treatment was discovered.

Cures are still being sought for the many medical conditions arising from another of Columbus's discoveries - tobacco. The use of tobacco has spread around the world more widely than any other drug. Columbus noted in his log that some of his sailors had seen natives indulging in a strange habit. So bewildering was the experience that he was not able to properly describe it. The Indians, he says, appeared to 'drink' the smoke from rolls of burning leaves which they collected from the plant called *nicotiana tabacum.* Today, every culture in the World has been introduced to some form of tobacco use. It is sometimes claimed that Sir Walter Raleigh introduced smoking into Britain. It is probably true to say that he was one of the first English gentlemen to take up the habit of smoking; but inhaling smoke was actually not unknown in the Old World. The fumes of coltsfoot and dried cow dung, in particular, were believed to be good for health, a way of warding off plague and curing headaches, asthma, gout, ulcers and even (ironically enough) cancer.

Tobacco, too, when it was introduced, was thought to promote health:

> 'Tobacco is found by good experience to help to spit out tough phlegm from the stomach, chest and lungs. The juice made into a syrup, or the smoke taken by a pipe helps to expel worms in the stomach and belly and the griping pains in the bowels. The seed is very effectual to expel the tooth ache, and the ashes of the burnt herb to cleanse the gums and make the teeth white. The juice is also used to kill lice in children's heads'.

[Nicholas Culpepper *Complete Herbal(1653)]*

In 1604 in England, King James I wrote a book against smoking, which he considered 'lothesome to the eye, hatefull to the Nose, harmfull

24. Columbus's men discover the Indians smoking tobacco
    [from Thevet *Singularitez* (1558)

to the braine, dangerous to the lungs...' Despite his criticisms, he did
acknowledge nicotine's extraordinary power as both a sedative and
calmer of nerves, on the one hand; and its effectiveness as a stimulant, on
the other:

> 'Being taken when they goe to bed, it makes one sleepe soundly, and yet
> being taken when a man is sleepie and drowsie, it will... awake his braine,
> and quicken his understanding'.

King James lost his fight against tobacco - the circulation of his trea-
tise obviously being limited at that time - and silver and clay pipes
became all the rage in the early seventeenth century. Cigars were also
smoked, but the habit did not really catch on then. Snorting tobacco as
snuff has also been fashionable at various times.

'Tobacco might be cultivated with advantage through the greater part
of Europe', suggested Adam Smith in his *Wealth of Nations (1776)*.
Certainly, governments all over the world today have sometimes found it
expedient to minimise the harmful effects of tobacco because of the considerable revenues which result from the sale of tobacco products.

Of all the merchandise brought back from the New World, tobacco
has arguably been the biggest curse; for, unlike syphilis, a cure for cancer
has yet to be discovered. Indeed, the most recent estimate is that in

Britain today the deaths of some three thousand people per week can be attributed to tobacco smoking; and in the world as a whole, it is reckoned that one person dies from tobacco smoking every thirteen seconds. The scale of these deaths has understandably given grounds for the belief that we are still paying a price for the achievements of Columbus and those who followed him in opening up the New World.

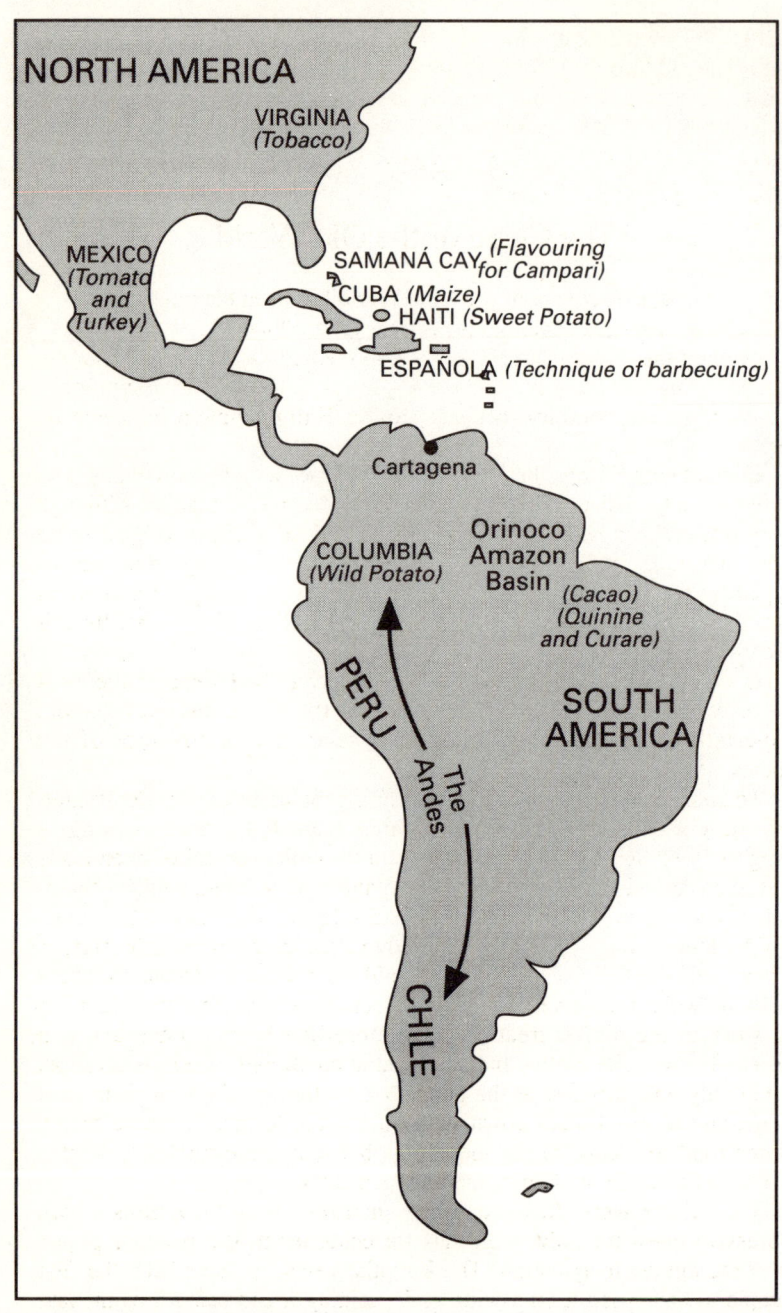

25. The origins of Columbus's legacy

Chapter XI

The Curse of the Old World

'The discovery of the New World has been the most
disastrous event in the history of mankind'
claimed the American philosopher, Cornelius De Pauw in 1768. He
was referring, particularly, to slavery - a reprehensible, barbaric practice
which ran quite contrary to the period of Enlightenment in which he
lived.

Contact with Europe, believed Columbus, would have a civilising, and
above all, a Christian influence on the native Indian population. Although
very few Indians were in fact cannibals, and all seemed to have some
kind of simple religion, they were nevertheless for a long while stereo-
typed by the Europeans as uncivilised heathens. Casting themselves as
'saviours', the conquerors would bring the Indians the gospel by fair
means or foul.

In reality, colonisation brought with it slavery and some of the most
barbaric treatments of native peoples that the world has ever known,
especially under Ovando, Columbus's successor as governor of the
Indies.

To some extent, the brutalities can be attributed to the decidedly mot-
ley crew which set sail with Columbus from Palos that morning in
August 1492. Some of the sailors, though fewer than has often been made
out, were convicted criminals from Spanish jails. Dehumanised themselves because of the treatment they had suffered, they had little sympa-
thy for these primitive peoples whom they considered to be their inferior.
They made the Indians sift grains of gold from the soil, threatening them
with the whip if they were too slow. Others took men from their families
to work in the mines, treating them more like beasts of burden than
human beings. The captive Indians lived in conditions of semi-starvation,
often only able to gnaw at the bones left by the Spaniards at their meal
table, and to grind them down with yucca root to make cassava bread.
Some tried to escape to the mountains but they were ruthlessly hunted
down and made to work in chains as a punishment.

The sailors were, however, only instruments in Columbus's own
obsessive quest for gold. Gold has for centuries held a peculiar power
over the human imagination. The Egyptians seem to have been the first
people to have used it on a wide scale, mining it and using it as money.
Spain's interest in gold arose after the Roman Conquest. Then, in the
tenth century, some gold reached Europe from Ghana in West Africa but

the output was disappointing. India, China and Japan all possessed gold but these countries absorbed it all themselves, and were too powerful for the Europeans to plunder.

When Columbus set foot on new lands in the Indies, finding gold was prominent amongst his objectives. His imagination was fuelled by tales of cities glittering with gold; of pieces of ore as large as a child's head; and of a king nearby - it was always nearby but always just beyond his grasp - who was served from gold dishes. The fact that he could find none of these things, far from frustrating him, seems merely to have made him the more resolved. Undeterred, he had feverishly ventured on from one island to the next in its pursuit: 'This island is very large and I decided to sail round it because as I understand, in or near it, there is a goldfield'. Other islands were only worth a brief visit precisely because 'they are so poor in gold'. By 1499, groups of natives under Spanish control were exploiting small quantities of gold in the sands and gravels of mountain streams. Little did Columbus know what his successors would find in the years to follow : the great riches of the Incas and Montezuma's treasure. Indeed, by 1600, the supply of precious metals in the world had increased by about eight times that at the time the Europeans had discovered America. It was beyond the understanding of the conquerors how the natives should attach no special value to gold and, if anything, preferred copper. Such trifles as tags, leather decorations and little bells seemed to be far more precious to them. Being unused to bartering, they simply accepted whatever the Spanish were prepared to exchange for them. This economic naivety had been noticed at San Salvador during the first voyage, when the crews offered the Indians broken crockery in return for generous quantities of cotton and what little gold they had.

Within a year, reported his son, Ferdinand, Columbus had marched through Española, reducing the Indians to obedience and making them promise to pay 'tribute' in gold to the King and Queen of Spain every three months. In the mountains of Cibao, where the gold mines were, every person of fourteen years old and upwards was to pay a large hawk's bell of gold dust; and people from other places were to pay twenty-five pounds of cotton as a tribute. When an Indian delivered his tribute, he received a brass or copper token which he had to wear about his neck as proof of payment. Any Indian found without one of these tokens was arrested and severely punished. These conditions were often quite impossible to meet, and many natives fled to the mountains in despair.

Columbus's desire for gold led directly to the expansion of slavery. Slavery had existed since the dawn of civilisation, and had reached its peak in Classical Greece and Rome. However, during the middle ages, it saw something of a decline, as bond men became free; but the lucrative slave trade had continued with Central Africa. Some of the negroes found their way to the markets of Western Europe, and tradition has it that

Columbus himself carried one or two negroes on his first voyage. Slavery also existed among the Indian tribes themselves: the Aztecs, for example, were used to enslaving outcasts and criminals; and Indians might well stake themselves as slaves should they lose when gambling. Nowhere, however, was slavery on a great scale: no tribe held another in a state of subjection and demanded servile labour from it.

Whether Columbus had slavery in mind all along is unclear. It seems more likely that, for him, the economic possibilities which it yielded grew and grew - his gold could rescue Jerusalem from the infidel. In order to achieve this aim, Columbus had no compunction against enslaving the native population. On one occasion, he coolly reported in his log that he had 'captured seven head of women, young ones and adults, and three small children'. Another time, he wrote to the King and Queen of Spain:

> 'In the name of the Holy Trinity, from here we can send as many slaves as can be sold... and if I am well informed, we might sell four thousand which would certainly be worth twenty million... and though they may die at first, it will not always be so, for the same happened with blacks and Canary-islanders at first...'

From the Spanish point of view, there could only be a sufficient labour supply if the natives were coerced into working. As it was, the conquerors' task seemed to be easy: these 'simple' people had only to be converted, and they would be prepared to co-operate with the Spanish.

In the Spring of 1494, Columbus shipped off five hundred slaves to Spain, where they were sold by auction in Seville. All of them soon died due to their harsh treatment and disease. Later cargoes of slaves, contrary to Columbus's firm expectations, also perished. The reaction of the King and Queen of Spain, was firmly against making their new Indian subjects into slaves. Isabella, in particular, demanded that they be well-treated and 'receive no injury in their persons or property'; and that all those slaves who had survived the hardships of the journey to Spain should be returned to Española, and be set free. Nevertheless, within little over ten years, the population of Española had been reduced by at least three-quarters.

Of the few contemporaries who were opposed to what Columbus was doing, one of the most outspoken was a Dominican friar called Antonio de Montesinos. In a Christmas sermon preached at Santo Domingo in 1511, he denounced the Spanish settlers:

> 'You are in mortal sin... for the cruelty and tyranny you see in dealing with these innocent people. Tell me, by what right or justice do you keep these Indians in such a cruel and horrible servitude? On what authority have you waged a detestable war against these people who dwelt quietly and peaceably on their own land?'... With the excessive work you demand of them

they fall ill and die, or rather you kill with your desire to extract and acquire gold every day'.

Montesinos's denunciation was rejected by Columbus's successor, Ovando, and he was made to return to Spain in 1515.

The Spanish bishop, Bartolomé de las Casas, continued to fight for the rights of the Indians. He was so horrified by what was happening to the Caribbean Indians that he personally pleaded for them at the Spanish Court. Later, in his book *The Tears of the Indians,* he gave an eye witness account of how the Spaniards had cruelly massacred more than twenty million people throughout the West Indies, Mexico and South America by 1550:

> 'To these quiet Lambs, embued with such blessed qualities, came the Spaniards like most cruel Tygres, Wolves, and Lions, enrag'd with a sharp and tedious hunger...'

The Spaniards took away women and children. They consumed in one day food sufficient for three Indian families of ten people each. 'Well armed with Sword and Launce', they destroyed cities and villages, the Indians having but bullrushes by comparison to defend themselves with. They ripped open the bellies of pregnant women, took out the tiny infants and hewed them into pieces. On other occasions, they killed both mother and child simultaneously with a single thrust of their swords. Children were taken by their feet, and their heads were dashed against rocks. Hands were half cut off, and lay dangling by flaps of skin. Whilst their leaders were roasted alive on specially made perches, others - arranged in groups of thirteen to represent Jesus and the twelve apostles - were burnt alive as they hung from the gallows. So much for the invaders' Christian impulses, writes Las Casas:

> '... from the beginning to this day, the Spaniards were never any more mindful to spread the Gospel among them, then as if they had been dogs...'

Las Casas's solution to the suffering of the American Indian was simply to replace him in the mines and on the plantations by more African slaves, who were already proving themselves good workers, and seemed to enjoy better health than the Indians. Over the next few years, the Portuguese - who had a large empire in Africa - provided some four thousand Africans for work in the New World.

Again, it is unjust to lay the blame entirely at Columbus's feet for the growth of slavery throughout the New World. Since he had not found anything like all the gold he had hoped for, slaves were his only way of paying for the cargoes of goods and livestock which arrived at Española every year. Few people at this time saw slavery with the kind of abhorrence with which we do today; and it was a well-established custom that any barbarous, infidel people (i.e. non-Christians) who were taken prisoners during war could legitimately be made slaves. On his deathbed, Columbus repeated that he had only intended that the Indians be taught Western customs and Christianity in Spain, and then be returned so as to teach others. As sincere a Christian as he was, he had failed to realise the probable long-term consequences of his actions, namely the spread of the horrors of slavery throughout the West Indies.

It is unfair to say that Columbus's motives were evil, and that it was his full intention from the very beginning to enslave the New World. Certainly, there were episodes in which he was involved, which to twentieth century eyes appear cruel - whether we are looking at the expedition which he launched against the defenceless Indians of Española; or in the mass slaughter and destruction of numerous villages. However, Columbus cannot reasonably be expected to have foreseen that these events should lead to the eventual extinction of the Arawaks and other tribes, together with the loss of their traditional cultures, until today the Indians are limited to a few reservations.

Out of slavery was born one of the most economically profitable ventures of the eighteenth century - the 'triangular' slave trade. Here, European cloth, trinkets and domestic hardware were sent to Africa in return for slaves. These slaves were then sent out to the West Indies as a cheap source of labour, to work in gangs in the sugar and tobacco plantations. In return, the West Indies supplied Europe with such items as silver, gold, drugs and tropical fruit. Britain came to be one of the principal European 'slavers', and cities such as Bristol and Liverpool prospered on the profits made from buying and selling human beings.

During the initial period of invasion and enslavement, Spain and other European countries destroyed native religions, society and culture in their quest for gold. Sparsely spread and disunited, the Indians were often quite unable to resist attacks from the Europeans, who decimated them with their diseases, and intensified Indian tribal warfare by supplying the Indians with horses and weapons.

The Indians had developed varied, and often fairly advanced cultures before the European conquests. They lived, for the most part, quietly and peaceably in communes. They were often artistic; and were uncorrupted by western standards, showing no desire to acquire wealth and land at the expense of their fellow tribesmen. In a material sense, they were 'very poor in everything', to use Columbus's own words; they had only domesticated the dog; they had no wheeled vehicles, plows or iron implements; and communicated by sign language. The Europeans, on the other hand, had ships and horses for transport, and fire-arms for protection. They could also communicate by writing. These cultures suffered at the hands of selfish white people who tended to see the Indians as lazy, deceitful and prone to vice.

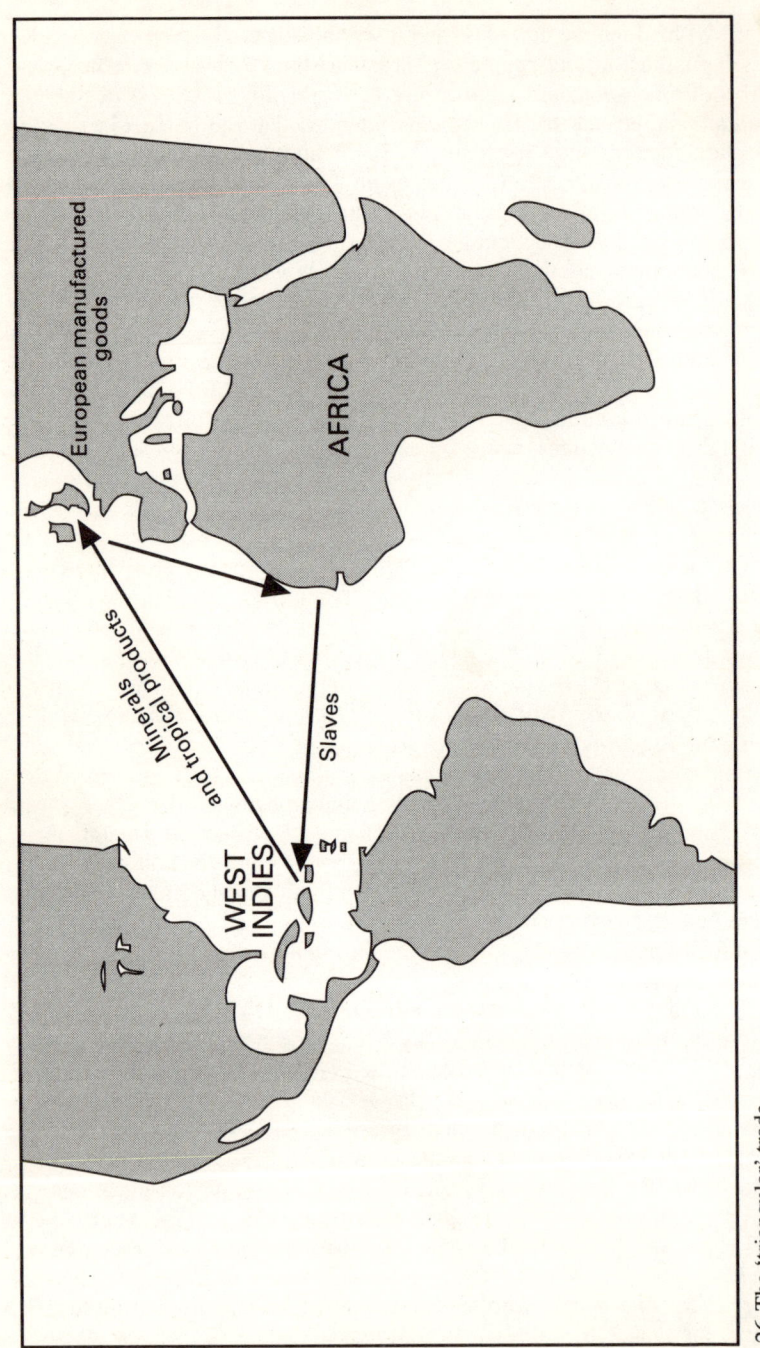

26. The 'triangular' trade

At first, Columbus believed that the American Indians were without any religion. In this, he was quite wrong - the Indians were very religious. Of the hundreds of tribal groups, most had a concept of god, of a supreme being. They also depended on a spirit world to explain the unexpected and incomprehensible: thunder and lightning, illness and death. When the Spanish imposed their own particular religion on the Indians, they were arrogantly assuming that the Indians were spiritually underdeveloped; and when they disturbed tribal religious practices, they were taking it for granted that the Catholic way of worship was the only true one.

The Old World not merely brought the curse of slavery, the destruction of life and property, and materialistic ideas at odds with traditional cultures; it also exported the means of self-destruction by introducing the sword and, worse, the gun to the Indians, who had hitherto been 'very unskilled in arms' [Columbus, 14 October, 1492]. The Indians' naivety concerning weapons was demonstrated clearly when the Spaniards showed the Indians their swords - for Europeans an ancient weapon - and they seized them by the blades, cutting themselves.

When Spain first became involved in overseas expansion, she transferred workers from casting bells to casting bronze guns; and from forging iron utensils to producing wrought iron cannon. Later, other Europeans such as the British and French gave the Indians arms for hunting, which led to tribes invading each others' territories on an unprecedented scale. The arrival of the rifle and the revolver led to a great many deaths among the Californian Indians in particular.

The introduction of the horse had an unforeseen effect in the use of fire-arms. Strictly speaking, Columbus reintroduced the horse, for there are abundant fossil remains to prove that horses were present in North America fifty million years ago. Horses were still numerous in North and South America when men first entered the New World from Asia some twenty thousand years ago. For some reason, which remains a mystery, the horse then became extinct. In Europe, during Julius Caesar's time, the horse was being domesticated. It was first used for war purposes, drawing chariots with army supplies. During the middle ages, the horse was rapidly developed in size to some seventeen or eighteen hands, capable of carrying a knight laden with heavy armour - a combined weight of four hundred pounds. It was by now a highly proficient running animal.

In 1493, on his second voyage, Columbus took with him twenty-four stallions, ten mares and three mules. More horses were sent from Spain with every fleet in the following years. The Spanish Crown then promoted their breeding by establishing (c.1498) royal farms in Española and neighbouring islands. The horse was then taken to Puerto Rico, Jamaica and finally to Cuba which was later to supply horses for Cortés's conquest of Mexico. Their first appearance had astonished the Indians, some of whom thought in the excitement and terror of the moment that horse and rider were a single animal. Two centuries later, the Indians began capturing Spanish horses. Now able to move around rapidly, their lifestyle changed from trudging foot-people to ferocious mobile buffalo-hunters and fighters; this immeasurably increased the amount of tribal warfare.

As the settlers swept across America, they brought the diseases of the Old World with them. Before they came, the Indians were physically a fit people, with many living to a hundred years old. They were free from the many scourges of the Old World, such as smallpox, measles, leprosy, scrofula and widespread tuberculosis, which the Indians came to call the 'cough demon'. Smallpox reached the already greatly diminished population of Española in 1518, sealing the fate of those who remained. In later centuries, it accounted for millions of deaths among the North American Indians, and some tribes in the Upper Missouri Valley were completely annihilated. It reached New England from the French before the time of the Pilgrim Fathers, and devastated Massachusetts. Almost simultaneously, a plague, possibly spread by European fishermen, ravaged the same area. Meanwhile, those Indians who were brought back to Mediterranean countries were quick to pick up Old World diseases. In many ways, disease had just as important a role to play in the submission of the Indians to the Europeans as did the fire-arm and the horse.

Before the invasions, the natives had no alcoholic beverages as we know them. Afterwards, they began to develop a craving for them. The introduction of alcohol ('stinking water', as the Indians called it) further increased the incidence of disease by undermining the health of the Indians. Tribal rulers adopted a similar stance towards alcohol as King James I had done towards tobacco - denouncing it completely, and handing out dire punishments (beatings to death and garrottings) to those who dared to drink it. The pre-Hispanic emperor of Mexico, Calderon Narvaez, declared that wine was:

> 'the root and source of all evil... the cause of all this discord and strife, and all the rebelliousness and restlessness among the people and kingdoms; it is like a whirlwind that stirs up and smashes everything... Drunkenness is the cause of all the adulteries, rapes, corruptions of virgins, and fights with relatives and friends; drunkeness is the cause of all the thefts and robberies and banditry and violence; it is also the cause of cursing and lying and gossip and slander, and of clamouring, quarrels, and shouting'.

When we examine the balance sheet of gains and losses in the conquest of the New World, it seems difficult to avoid the conclusion that the many voyages of exploration which followed that of Columbus produced more benefits for the Old World than they did for the New. We have much to thank the New World for; but in return we gave these people relatively little of lasting value. In the same way that the early conquerors took advantage of the Indians by exchanging their broken crockery for gold, so the Old World has continued to exploit the resources of the New when the opportunity has arisen - whether it be in the physical environment or in the workplace.

27. The first bronze statue of Columbus in the U.S.A., Tower Grove Park, St. Louis, Missouri

BIBLIOGRAPHY

PRIMARY SOURCES

Barwick, G.F. (ed.) *Christopher Columbus. His Own Book of Privileges,*
1502 (London, 1893)

Benzoni, G. *La Historia del Mondo Nuovo* (Venice, 1563)

Brooks, V.W. (ed.) *Christopher Columbus : the Journal of the first
Voyage to America* (Jarrolds, London, 1925)

Cohen, J.M. (ed.) *The Four Voyages of Columbus* (Selection of documents) (Cresset, London, 1969)

Dunn, O. and Kelly, J.E. (eds) *The Diario of Christopher Columbus's
First Voyage to America 1492-1493*
(University of Oklahoma Press, 1989)

Jane, C. (ed.) *The Journal of Christopher Columbus* (The Hakluyt
Society, London, 1960)

Keen, B. (ed.) *The Life of the Admiral Christopher Columbus by his son
Ferdinand* (Rutgers University Press, New Brunswick,
New Jersey, 1959)

Las Casas, B. de *The Tears of the Indians* (1656)

Las Casas, B. de *An Account of the First Voyages and Discoveries made
by the Spaniards in America* (1699)

Las Casas, B. de *The Log of Christopher Columbus's first voyage to
America in the year 1492* (W. H. Allen, London, 1944)

Latham, R. (ed.) *The Travels of Marco Polo* (Penguin, Harmondsworth,
1978)

Major, R.H. (ed.) S*elect Letters of Christopher Columbus* (The Hackluyt
Society, London, 1847)

Morison, S.E. (ed.) *Journals and other documents on the life and voyages
of Christopher Columbus* (Heritage, New York, 1963)

Oviedo, G.F. de *Historia general de las Indias* (Seville, 1535)

Seymour, M.C. (ed.) *The metrical version of Mandeville's Travels* (O.U.P., London, 1973)

SECONDARY SOURCES

Adams, C.K. 'Some Recent Discoveries concerning Columbus', *Annual Report of the American Historical Association* (1891) 89-99

Booth, N. 'On Course to fathom a mystery of the sea', *The Guardian* 22 November 1991

Bradford, E. *Christopher Columbus* (Michael Joseph, London, 1973)

Collis, J.S. *Christopher Columbus* (Sphere Books, London, 1989)

Cummins, J. (ed.) *The Voyage of Christopher Columbus* (Weidenfeld & Nicolson, London, 1992)

David, M. *Who was "Columbus?"* (The New York Research Publishing Company, 1933)

Davies, H. *In Search of Columbus* (Sinclair-Stevenson, London, 1991)

Duff, C. *The Truth about Columbus and the Discovery of America* (Jarrolds, London, 1957)

Dyson, J. and Christopher, P. *Columbus - For Gold, God and Glory* (Hodder & Stoughton, London, 1991)

Fernández-Armesto, F. *Columbus and the conquest of the impossible* (Weidenfeld and Nicolson, London, 1974)

Fernández-Armesto, F. *Before Columbus : Exploration and Colonisation from the Mediterranean to the Atlantic, 1229-1492* (Macmillan Education, 1987)

Fernández-Armesto, F. *Columbus* (Oxford University Press, 1992)

Fuson, R.H. *The Log of Christopher Columbus* (Ashford Press, Southampton, 1987)

Giardini, C. *The Life and times of Columbus* (Hamlyn, London, 1968)

Granzotto, G. *Christopher Columbus, The Dream & the Obsession* (Grafton Books, London, 1988)

Helps, A. *Christopher Columbus* (Everyman, 1910)

Houben, H.H. *Christopher Columbus. The Tragedy of a Discoverer* (Routledge, London, 1935)

Irving, W. *The Life and Voyages of Christopher Columbus; together with the voyages of his Companions* (Routledge, London, 1850)

Landstrom, B. *The Story of Don Cristóbal Colón* (Macmillan, New York, 1966)

Litvinoff, B. *Fourteen Ninety Two: the Year and the Era* (Constable, 1991)

Madariaga, S. de *Christopher Columbus, Being the Life of The Very Magnificent Lord Don Cristobal Colón* (Hodder & Stoughton, London, 1939)

Massie, A. 'The Sailor of the ocean blue', *The Sunday Telegraph*, 26 May 1991

Merrien, J. *Christopher Columbus : The Mariner and the Man* (Odhams Press, London, 1958)

Morison, S.E. *Admiral of the Ocean Sea : A Life of Christopher Columbus* (Oxford University Press, 1942)

Olsen, J.E. and Bourne, E.G. (eds) *The Northmen, Columbus and Cabot, 985-1503* (Barnes & Noble, New York, 1934)

Paolucci, A. and H. (eds) *Columbus.Selected Papers on Columbus and his Time* (Council on National Literatures, Whitestone, New York, 1989)

Phillips, W. D. and Phillips, C. R. *The Worlds of Christopher Columbus* (Cambridge University Press, 1992)

Russell, J. 'Inventing the Flat Earth', *History Today* (August 1991) 13-13-19

Sale, K. *The Conquest of Paradise. Christopher Columbus and the Columbian Legacy* (Hodder & Stoughton, London, 1991)

Thacher, *J.B. Christopher Columbus: His Life, His Works, His Remains* (G.P.Putnam, New York and London, 1903)

Vorsey, L. de and Parker, J. *In the Wake of Columbus. Islands and Controversey (*Wayne State University Press, Detroit, 1985)

Weatherford, J . *Indian Givers* (Fawcett Columbine, New York, 1988)

Wilford, J. N. ' Experts Debate Theory on Columbus', *The New York Times,* 3 Nov. 1986

INDEX

sea-monsters 1, 3, 5
unicorns 1
Monte Cristi 50, 51, 62, 65, 73
Montesinos, Antonio de 117-118
Montezuma, Emperor 108
Montserrat 61, 74
moon, eclipse of 69, 95, 98,
Moors 30, 80, 85
Moslems 27
Moya, Beatrice de 20
Müller, Johannes 95

N

Naples, Lombard portrait of Columbus 9
Narvaez, Calderon 122
navigation theory 4-5
Nevri 15
Newfoundland 6
New World, the, effects of the conquest of 105-123
Niña (caravel) 30, 32, 33, 36, 39, 44, 47, 48, 50, 51, 57
Noroña, Don Martín de 55
Northern Ocean 2
North Pole 3
Norway 8
Nuestra Señora, Mar de 43

O

Odemira 72
olives 87
Orejas, Costa de las 87, 99
Orinoco-Amazon basin 108, 114
Oro, River 51, 64, 65
Ovando, Don Nicolás de 82, 86, 95, 96, 98, 115, 118
Oviedo, Gonzalo Fernández de 10, 105, bibliography

P

Palos 30, 47, 52, 55, 56
Paradise 1
Paria
gulf and coast of 77, 79, 83, 84
Boca del Dragon 77
passion fruit 109
Pauw, Cornelius de 115
Pavia, University of 16
peanuts 109
pearls 77
peppers 107
Peraza, Hernan 21
Perestrello, Bartolomeo 20

Perestrello, Felipa Moniz 19-20, 29
Pérez, Fray Juan 30
Piacenza 13
pineapple 109
Pinos, Bridge of 30
Pinta (caravel) 30, 31, 32, 36, 37, 48, 50, 52, 57
Pinzón, family 59
Martín Alonso 24, 30, 31, 32, 33, 34, 36, 37, 43, 50-51, 52, 56, 57
Vicente Yáñez 30, 37, 48
pirates 3
Pisa 4
pneumonia (*see* illness)
Polo, Marco 2
Pontevedra (Galicia) 15
Porras, Francisco 94, 96, 98
Portolans (*see* maps)
Porto Santo (Madeira) 20, 29, 75
Portugal 13, 16
potato 105-107, 114
Prester John 26
printing 2
Ptolemy, Claude 2
Puerto Bello (Panama) 89, 93, 98, 99,
Puerto Beuno (Jamaica) 93, 99
Puerto Grande 65
Puerto Retrete 90, 99
Puerto Rico illus. 74, 99
Punta del Arenal 76-77, 83
Punta de la Playa 76

Q

Queen's Garden 66
Quibián 91, 92
quinine 110, 114
Quintanilla, Alonso de 29
Quintero, Cristobál 31
Quiribirí 88, 98, 99

R

Raleigh, Sir Walter 106
Restello 55
rhubarb 48, 50, 109
Riega, García de la 15
Rinck portrait of Columbus 9-10
Roaring Forties 5
Roldán, Francisco 78-79, 80
Rum Kay/Cay (*see* Santa María de la Concepción)

S

St Brandan island 1
St Christopher 25, 26

Christopher Columbus